Sharing Your
Church Building

Sharing Your Church Building

Ralph D. Curtin

Baker Books

A Division of Baker Book House Co
Grand Rapids, Michigan 49516

© 2002 by Ralph D. Curtin

Published by Baker Books
a division of Baker Book House Company
P.O. Box 6287, Grand Rapids, MI 49516-6287

Printed in the United States of America

Library of Congress Cataloging-in-Publication Data

Curtin, Ralph D., 1944–
    Sharing your church building / Ralph D. Curtin.
      p.   cm.
    Includes bibliographical references.
    ISBN 0-8010-9144-6 (pbk.)
    1. Church buildings. 2. Cooperative ministry. I. Title.
    BV636 .C87 2002
    254′ .7—dc21   2002009995

For current information about all releases from Baker Book House, visit our web site:
                http://www.bakerbooks.com

To my helpmate and companion, Kathy, who has been a continuous source of edification during the good years and a pillar of strength and encouragement throughout the difficult years.

To the faithful pastor who explores the uncharted land of sharing his church, I, along with Paul, salute you: "Therefore, my dear brothers, stand firm. Let nothing move you. Always give yourselves fully to the work of the Lord, because you know that your labor in the Lord is not in vain" (1 Cor. 15:58).

Contents

Acknowledgments

The following contributors were among those who offered significant suggestions and critical advice to bring about the completion of this work. I am indebted to these workers whose labors, along with their prayers, made it all possible: Dr. Gary G. Cohen, professor emeritus, Trinity College and Trinity Evangelical Divinity School; Dr. Robert E. Coleman, director of School of World Missions and Evangelism and professor of Evangelism at Trinity Evangelical Divinity School; Dr. Dan Southerland, senior pastor of Flamingo Road Church, Davie, Florida.

Other principal workers who volunteered their time include Theona Cooke, assistant to the pastor at North Pompano Baptist Church, and Jacque Brown, a noble supporter.

Introduction

For the past several years, I have had the joyful experience of being the pastor of a church that shares its buildings with two other Christian groups. During this period, a wonderful interaction among leaders, staff, and laypersons of three separate nationalities has emerged that has greatly contributed to the depth of my ministry. There have been many lessons that have been learned through this journey, and this book is like a diary that chronicles that journey. My prayer is that this record will serve as a ministry resource to any pastor or Christian leader who is presently engaged in sharing his or her church, or contemplating the unique undertaking for the future.

This book is designed to provide fresh insight into the management of sharing your church with other groups of like faith without sacrificing the identity of your own congregation. The issue of sharing your church is relevant for today because vast numbers of churches are experiencing dwindling membership and proportionately vacant rooms, rendering their church facilities prime candidates to share with other ministries. Also, there are many emerging groups that believe God's calling is to begin a church, and they are searching for a nonhostile environment, a place of worship and fellowship, that will accommodate them until they are able to manage on their own. I will endeavor to show why God would want you to share your church with these struggling groups, even though sharing buildings and expenses can bring with it many headaches. I believe these headaches are blessings in disguise. In fact, sharing your church with other ministries should be a blessing.

This book may be used as a reference tool that will assist any host church to receive God's best by encouraging the right attitude toward solving the problems that come when tenants, be they American or multiethnic, share the facility. It provides an up-to-date ministry guide to assist the host church's decision-making process, as well as the daily operation for the care of guest groups.

Although this work is presented from a Baptist perspective, my research draws from other denominations as well. You will see that the biblical principles and policies explained herein can be applied to every ministry (with variations according to sect) that is interested in sharing its church.

Also, from the guest church perspective, practical advice is given on when to consider moving and what you should look *for* and look *at* when considering a rental relationship with an established ministry. Further, to aid in the decision-making process, I have dealt with the question of whether you should rent space in a building or a nearby church.

Sharing Your Church Building warrants presentation from both the host and guest perspective. It is my duty before God to approach this subject in such a way as to protect both of these parties from harm. Accordingly, when we discuss buildings, structural renovations, signs, boundaries, and covenants that pertain to finances and church polity, my goal is always to promote ongoing reconciliation between the brethren while making a profound statement to the world that Christians can live and worship together in unity.

Rev. Ralph D. Curtin, D. Min.
Sunrise, Florida

1

Why Should You Share
Your Church?

I was on the job as the new senior pastor of the North Pompano Baptist Church only one week when the "field reports" started coming in. My secretary received a phone call from an inquiring homemaker in the community who asked what the status of our church was since many people in the neighborhood thought from the outside look of the church that it was closed. Rumors that our church was really a Brazilian church or a Haitian church followed. The residents in the nearby vicinity didn't know what kind of church we offered or whether we were indeed operating as an American church. It became apparent to me that my first task as the new pastor was to clearly define who we were and with whom we were sharing our church.

Within two weeks' time I learned the history of our church and realized the course of events that led up to the decision to bring two other church groups into our fold. The church facilities consisted of an original two-hundred-seat sanctuary built in the late 1950s and a newer seven-hundred-seat sanctuary built in the 1970s along with a two-hundred-seat fellowship hall and a large two-wing education building, consisting of twenty classrooms, on six acres of land. These facilities fell into disrepair several years earlier mainly because of dwindling finances due to departing members. Economic change in the surrounding neighborhood was another contributing factor.

I discovered that a number of years ago the church leadership agreed to share the buildings with both the Brazilian and Haitian ministries in an effort to assist them—giving them an opportunity to start their churches—while bringing in extra revenue to defray expenses at the same time. A loving idea, but due to unforeseen circumstances, namely, extraordinary guest group growth, adjustments in the host-guest relationship would be needed. By the time I began my ministry at NPBC five years later, the size of the Brazilian church, now boasting a membership of more than 700 members (the largest Brazilian church in America as of this writing), and a Haitian ministry of more than 125 members began to intimidate the decreasing American membership to the degree that many of the Americans were persuaded that the Brazilian church had taken over the entire facility and the other two groups (American and Haitian) were now the guest groups.

By virtue of its burgeoning size, the Brazilian church constantly needed more room to expand. It quickly swallowed up all the spaces in the parking lot and occupied nearly all the vacant rooms while scheduling the sanctuary and fellowship hall with activities that eclipsed the American church. Without a written agreement in place to protect the American congregation from being overrun, the American church would soon lose its sovereignty. This caused more people to leave.

Finances then became even more critical for the American church. In time, the Brazilian church purchased a sizeable piece of acreage of the American church property to build a multipurpose building. So by the time my ministry began at this church, the Brazilian and Haitian churches were firmly entrenched and resolved to stay. However, the American church was in trouble.

In one of my favorite Peanuts cartoons, Lucy demands that Linus change TV channels and then threatens him with her fist if he doesn't.
"What makes you think you can walk right in here and take over?" asks Linus.
"These five fingers," says Lucy. "Individually they're nothing but when I curl them together like this into a single unit, they form a weapon that is terrible to behold."
"Which channel do you want?" asks Linus.
Turning away, he looks at his fingers and says, "Why can't you guys get organized like that?"
—Bruce Shelley, "What Is the Church?"

Both the Brazilian and Haitian churches possessed well-structured leadership, but there was no organization to bring the three ministries together. Soon after my arrival I knew the Lord had brought me to NPBC to bring about both the organization and clarity of the identity of all three congregations, because the negative voices crying "confusion" in the neighborhood troubled me. I wanted our church to make a statement to the community that we should share our buildings because unity is a good testimony (John 17:23). But, obviously, some clarity needed to be brought to the situation.

Shared Ministry

One day it dawned on me that the mind of the Lord is to share ministry, to use the facilities he has provided for their maximum potential and serve him. "How good and pleasant it is when brothers live together in unity!" (Ps. 133:1). This provided a platform for me to embrace both of the guest pastors since I could not maintain an attitude of isolation by thinking our facility was just for Americans or English-speaking people. Whatever inconveniences we would suffer would be outweighed by the blessings of proclaiming the gospel with a united front.

Unity

First I dealt with the issue of *unity* and the reason we should share our church from an academic perspective. G. W. Bromiley writes:

> The word unity is very rare in the Bible, but the thought behind the term, that of the one people of God, is extremely prominent. In the New Testament this unity is expanded in accordance with the original promise. The wall of partition between Jew and Gentile, and indeed between Greek and barbarian, bond and slave, male and female is broken down. There is now the one people of God embracing men of all nations (Eph. 2:12–13; Gal. 3:28). . . . The one Jesus Christ is the basis of the unity of his people. . . . As divided men they first meet in his crucified body, in which their old life is put to death and destroyed. They are reconciled in one body by the cross (Eph. 2:16). . . . Believers have their new life in Christ as they are all born of the one Spirit (John 3:5; Eph. 4:4). . . . But this means that they are all brothers of Jesus Christ and of one another in the one family of God. They are led by the one Spirit, being built up as a habitation of God through the Spirit (Eph. 2:22). . . . Since it is by faith that Christians belong to Christ, their unity is a unity of faith (Eph. 4:13). . . . Christian unity is not identical with uniformity. It does not allow division. But it does not exclude variety. . . . The unity grounded in Christ leaves scope for diversity of action and function, the only conformity being to the mind of Christ and direction of the Spirit.[1]

God's Command

My research brought me to the conclusion that *we should share our church* because the Word of God declares it. If that were not enough, when we look at the early church and how it shared everything in common, we see that the Lord greatly blessed it (Acts 2:42–47). The wall of partition between nationalities had been broken down through Christ and the people were obedient to the Word; therefore, God blessed. As far as the problems that come with sharing—if the leadership were submissive to the Holy Spirit—I had every confidence that any concerns would be resolved in time.

I believed God wanted us to share our facilities because we had large quarters with available or unused space that could be rotated for other ministries. But uppermost in my mind was maintaining our identity without giving away the store. What was needed was a meeting with each of the guest pastors to see where their hearts were in relationship to the host church. As it turned out, this meeting only fortified the Word of God in my heart. These pastors were truly men of God. Their design was in no way to threaten the integrity of our church. They were very grateful for the opportunity to develop their ministry while coming under the roof of the American church.

Still, we needed to define who we were and who they were. Their method of worship was different from ours. There were language barriers. There were cultural differences. But despite these barriers, their zeal for the Lord—their prayer warriors, their praise and worship teams, their indomitable spirit to survive and thrive in America while being a testimony for their God, our God—seemed to say to me that I needed to be their friend. I needed to convey unity and understanding to these sojourners in a foreign land and respect them. Once we, the pastors, respected one another, that respect filtered down into the congregations.

Who's Who

Next, I set out to clarify who we were and with whom we were sharing our church. My calling was to the American church; therefore it was incumbent on me and the other pastors not to combine all three churches into one ministry. We wanted to celebrate our life in Christ together but not at the expense of blending and straining our heritages. Other churches have merged their guest groups into one membership, but after careful consideration and consultation with the other pastors I believed it was apparent that we were not to go in that direction.

Looking to the Old Testament, we see that the twelve tribes had a similar understanding. They were all of the nation of Israel, all believing in the same God, coming to worship together on the prescribed holy days, yet remaining individual tribes. When we applied this philosophy at NPBC, it worked for us. Because we are of the same faith and denomination, many of the biblical or doctrinal issues are nonexistent. This made it easier to accommodate one another. So when it came to rotating our scheduling of the sanctuary for worship services, the fellowship hall, many of the classrooms, the outside pavilions, and the playground, it was achieved with a joyful spirit.

With the fundamentals in place, we set out to make the renovations on the buildings. Extensive work was required to bring the church, appurtenant structures, and grounds up to an acceptable level (this is discussed in more detail in chapter 5). Naturally, since the buildings dated back to the fifties and seventies, there was a limit to what could be improved. But, nevertheless, the gradual renovations and repairs proved to the community that the church was very much alive. After only six months of refurbishing, the church became a front-page story in a local newspaper; the article discussed the church's renovations and its positive impact on the community.

As the repairs progressed (laying down a new carpet in the sanctuary was a biggie!), the spirit of the people in the congregation began to rebound. With renewed interest, the American people in the community reemerged to see what God was doing back at their church. This eventually led to greater numbers, adding financial support to our ministry, and after one year, for the first time in several years, NPBC met its budget.

Current Trend to Share Churches in Florida

Of the 163 Southern Baptist churches and missions in Broward County, Florida, 36 percent are sharing their church facilities with another nationality. Nationally, there are hundreds of churches that are sharing their facilities with Hispanics, Asians, Europeans, and scores of other nationalities. This seems to indicate that many churches are finding themselves with available space, and rather than use it for storage or let it remain empty, they are opting to share it with another ministry.

If Florida, with its constant influx of immigrants from the Caribbean and South America, is a representative slice of the national average, it is apparent that the people of yesterday's mission fields are now relocating to America's shores and towns. Indeed, Florida's Broward County is home to eighty-six language groups that make up the various multicultural congregations sprouting up all over the southern part of the Sunshine State. This continuous infusion of people from other lands provides a wonderful opportunity for mission churches to branch out.

When the leadership of your church spreads its outreach wings and embraces other ministries, in time, your church will see the need to share your facility with other Christian works that require space. In addition to hosting the Brazilian and Haitian ministries at NPBC, we also accommodate Trinity International University, which sets up a satellite campus on our premises once a week. We also welcomed Moody Bible Institute to our facility as well as the Boy Scouts of America and the Hope Crisis Pregnancy Ministry, a Christ-centered ministry dedicated to unwed mothers in our region. In doing this, we have taken the word *unity* to a higher level in ministry.

General Principles Apply to All

Back in 1973 a Jewish-Christian woman prayed with me at a home Bible study to receive Christ as my Savior. After several years our evangelical Messianic Jewish fellowship progressed to a storefront ministry that ultimately led to a building of our own, where we conducted our outreach and church activities for several more years. Then God moved me and my family to a moderately sized independent Baptist church. Due to ministry opportunities, we then joined a large, seeker-friendly church. Shortly afterward, I attended an Evangelical-Free Bible college and graduate school, followed by a Pentecostal seminary, where I received my doctorate degree. For the past six years I have been teaching for both Trinity College (Evangelical-Free, nondenominational) and Moody Bible Institute, a nondenominational school. In all of my ministry experience and research, which includes discussing the material in this book with other denominational pastors and fellow professors from various churches, one thing is very clear: The principles I've discovered and explained in this book are relevant to all Christian groups, regardless of their geographical location or ecclesiastical polity.

2

United We Stand

After serving at NPBC for several months, I began to realize we had a major problem—our congregation was not really growing. Sure, our buildings were being refurbished and rebuilt, but our membership was not. In reflection, I believe it is more difficult to rebuild a ministry than it is to start a new one.

As to the cause, my hunch was that many of the former members, along with the immediate community, were slowly being transplanted into other churches. It occurred to me that perhaps they were turned off by rumors concerning our church's acquisition of different ministries. After careful consideration, I decided to visit a nearby church of the same denomination to ask the pastor for help in rebuilding our ministry. His congregation was very large, so my plan was to ask him for ten committed couples who would want to serve the Lord at our church for one year, a short-term "missionary adventure," if you will. Naturally, their absence would not endanger their home church since it was a well-established and flourishing ministry. Of course, their financial support would continue to their home church.

I believed such a plan would help staff some of our vacancies. Our Sunday school and youth group needed teachers.

Visitors would see a larger, varied congregation that they could relate to. This would engender the attitude that we were a growing church and inject some vitally needed "new blood" into our congregation—new people bring a renewed spirit and interest in the work of God. But it was not meant to be.

At our meeting, much to my disappointment and surprise, the pastor said, "I could never get my deacons to approve of that idea."

In my heart and mind, we were of the same faith, and even the same denomination, so why not help out a fellow pastor and sister church—especially when we proclaim unity in the body of Christ. This meeting, as discouraging as it was, catapulted me to new heights. I resolved to press on despite this setback. I would trust the Lord to build up his church in whatever way he saw fit. The incident, however, did remind me of an observation by James S. Hewett:

> We will never become a church that effectively reaches out to those who are missing out if we shoot our wounded and major on the minuses. . . . Next fall when you see geese heading south for the winter, flying along in a V formation, you might be interested in knowing what science has discovered about why they fly that way. It has been learned that as each bird flaps its wings, it creates an uplift for the bird immediately following. By flying in a V formation, the whole flock adds at least 71 percent greater flying range than if each bird flew on its own. (Christians who share a common direction and a sense of community can get where they are going quicker and easier, because they are traveling on the thrust of one another.)
>
> Whenever a goose falls out of formation, it suddenly feels the drag and resistance of trying to go it alone, and quickly gets back into formation to take advantage of the lifting power of the bird immediately in front. (If we have as much sense as a goose, we will stay in formation with those who are headed the same way we are going.)[1]

Shortly afterward I met with the Brazilian pastor, who agreed with me that God would build his church apart from human instrumentality. We jointly renewed the vision for our church, then went on to bind our relationship in Christ. It was Aesop who said, "United we stand, divided we fall," but God spoke to the apostle Paul centuries later and made the motto into a precept when he said, "Make every effort to keep the unity of the Spirit through the bond of peace" (Eph. 4:3).

J. Campbell White prescribes four things that bind people together: common hope, common work, deliverance from a common peril, and loyalty to a common friend.[2] We had three out of the four. Our common hope was for our ministries to grow, our ministering for Christ was our common work, and we were both loyal to one another (and the cause of Christ as well). The only peril that loomed on the horizon was unbelief, and that enemy would be kept at bay with constant prayer and our mutual drive and resolve to go forward in ministry despite any obstacles.

This mutual drive to go forward in ministry despite roadblocks comes out of one's love for the Lord and from love for one another. In our leadership, that love has brought a deep respect for each other's ministry that brings great harmony to the dispute table. When there is a dispute that arises in any of the three ministries in our church, we, as the pastors, sit down together and hash out the difficulty. Our belief is elementary: If there is love and harmony in the leadership, we can and do expect it in the rank-and-file. Our three ministries are not like individual ships passing in the night; they are united in purpose. Paul explains in Romans 15:30 that we, as a church, must strive together, exhorting us as a body to come together in unity against the common adversary— not to work against one another.

Unity within Denomination

Doctrinal differences can lead to disunity. This is why, in my experience, when sharing your church building, the host must insist that the guest ministry be of the same denomination. That would mean that Southern Baptists can easily embrace other Baptists, including GARB (General Association of Regular Baptist) churches. However, a Catholic church would not be a good fit for a Missionary Baptist group looking for a facility to start a church, due to divergent doctrines. Christian Reformed churches, while agreeing on Christ for salvation as the Baptists do, do not agree on eschatology, among other issues. While these may not be serious points of contention, inasmuch as the denominations agree on the major points of theology, they can cause problems in time, so why ask for trouble when there are enough groups in your own denomination looking for space to rent.

It can be debated at this point that doctrinal differences between a conservative evangelical church in the Christian Reformed denomination and a conservative Southern Baptist church do not matter. Some see a problem only when moral issues such as homosexuality, abortion, or church discipline between the two groups are disputed. In those cases, the disparity should then dictate that a sharing arrangement would not be feasible.

While this is a valid argument, I maintain that denominational differences in doctrine (Calvinism v. Arminianism, for instance) do indeed filter down into ethics, which can play a central role in the joint operation of both the host and guest churches.

Embracing this position, Paul writes, "I appeal to you, brothers, in the name of our Lord Jesus Christ, that all of you agree with one another so that there may be no divisions among you and that you may be *perfectly united in mind and thought"* (1 Cor. 1:10, italics mine). I believe the phrase *perfectly united* has been divinely inserted for a reason.

Friedrich Hanck adds,

> Christ, it is true, prayed "that they may all be one . . . just as We are one" (John 17:21–22 NASB); nevertheless the basis upon which union is being fostered must be examined. Any unity founded upon the joining of those who truly believe Christ is the only begotten Son of God, who became incarnate, died on the cross to bear the sins of the believer, and rose in a resur-

rected body on the third day, with men or churches which do not believe these fundamentals of the faith, is unscriptural.[3]

You might say that there are no boundaries in the church of God if we hold to the same basic doctrines. Not true. While there is neither Greek nor Jew in the church, but all are looked upon as one (Gal. 3:28), there are opposing views to certain biblical ordinances that must be evaluated. For instance, let us say that the potential guest church agrees with the host church on all points of doctrine noted above, but disagrees with your position against ordaining women into the pastorate. Or, your guest church has adopted the policy that they will appoint homosexuals to leadership as the situation arises. This mind-set will most certainly find its way into your church. To engage in a union of this kind could prove to be a disaster for your church.

Purpose for Unity in the Church

The foundation for unity in the church must be built on our love for Christ. It is that love for him which moves the church to spiritual oneness and combats such adversaries as Conor Cruise O'Brien (the Irish diplomat and writer), who stated, "Nothing does more to activate Christian divisions than to talk about Christian unity."[4]

Building on the foundation of our mutual love for Christ is the three-point superstructure for unity:

1. Unity in the church testifies to the unbelieving world that Christ came to provide salvation to all who would believe, "that all of them may be one, Father, just as you are in me and I am in you. . . . so that the world may believe that you have sent me" (John 17:21). When the lost world sees unity in the church, it is a dynamic testimony to God.
2. Unity in the church encourages the body of Christ while promoting joy through like-mindedness (Phil. 2:1–2).

The united church presents a united front in its witness of Christ.

3. Unity in the church exhibits the fruit of the Spirit, namely, love. "May they be brought to complete unity to let the world know that you sent me and have loved them even as you have loved me" (John 17:23). "When the world sees love flowing from the church, it sees the kind of love the Father has for Christ. It is a great comfort for believers to know that in a hostile world, the Father loves them as He does the Son."[5]

A Workable Strategy

Your Church Defined

The English term *church* comes from the Greek *kuriakon*, which is the neuter adjective of *kurios*, "Lord," and means "belonging to the Lord." In the New Testament the English word *church* is used to translate the Greek word *ekklesia*, which means "to call out." Putting these two meanings together, we come up with the following definition of church: a called-out local body or assembly of all those who profess faith and allegiance to Christ (1 Thess. 1:1; 1 Cor. 4:17; Gal. 1:22; Acts 15:14).

Ralph D. Winter comments on that application of church to unity:

> Granting that we have this rich diversity, let us foster unity and fellowship between congregations just as we now do between families rather than to teach everyone to worship like Anglo-Americans. . . . Let us glory in the fact that the world Christian family now already includes representatives of more different languages and cultures than any other organization or movement in human history.[6]

The modern church must be prepared to embrace and share its church building with others of like faith.

Written Resolution

Unity in the church is a biblical injunction, but sharing your church is a matter for the pastor and his board of deacons or the elected board to decide. Whether or not the decision is made by the congregation, the people of the church must be kept in the loop; they should know what is going on, and their concerns should be heard. This will help alleviate any potential problems. Once the decision is approved, you may consider adding a written resolution into your mission statement that will serve as a reminder of your church's ongoing efforts to adhere to the Great Commission. It will also serve as a compass for the evangelical outreach of your church.

Regular Meetings

Written agreements are not enough to maintain unity between congregations that share a church. Regular meetings between pastors are required to keep the lines of communication open. Scheduled meetings will help dissipate distrust and generate the image that the leadership is indeed united. This is vital for the welfare of both the host and guest churches. Naturally, scheduled meetings should involve staff personnel, deacons, and lay leaders and ensure continued cooperation among the congregations. By meeting each week with your guest pastors, you encourage unity. Regular weekly breakfast or luncheon appointments will do wonders to break down any walls that may have been inadvertently erected during the previous week.

Such was the case in our church when a delicate situation arose. The Brazilian pastor asked me for more classroom space to conduct activities for his ever-expanding ministry. At the present time their ministry occupies more than 25 percent of our facility space, the Haitian church, 25 percent, and NPBC, 25 percent, the remainder being common (we rotate usage). For me to allow him more space would seriously hamper any future growth of our American church and intimidate our congregation. Therefore, my position was to refuse him. Ordinarily, this would have caused a rift between pastors and the conflict would have filtered down to the congregations. But since the Brazilian pastor and I have an ongoing relationship, enhanced by our mutual respect for one another and augmented by our scheduled meetings, the refusal was quickly overlooked. Shortly afterward, the Brazilian pastor told me that he had taken care of the situation by arranging for portable classrooms to solve the dilemma.

The other pastors may speak different languages, have different approaches to ministry, and have different goals for their people, but when it comes to the great things of God—upholding the inerrant Word to reach the souls of men—fortunately, we agree with one another.

Cooperative Ministries

The example of cooperation in the leadership is quickly followed by the membership in various branches of ministry. Speaking through an interpreter, I have had the opportunity of sharing biblical truth with both the Brazilian and Haitian congregations. Naturally, receiving biblical truth from a different preacher from his unique perspective brings depth to the overall ministry. By bringing in one of your guest pastors or their associate pastors to the pulpit, you can allow them to share a message from God that you as the host pastor have been avoiding or have been reticent to approach. If your congregation has been experiencing a period of discouragement, and you as the pastor have been discouraged, another preacher might rekindle the flames to bring the ministry back on track.

Sharing musical talents between congregations not only is a marvelous testimony to the community, but also is a great enhancement of your musical capabilities. In our ministry at NPBC, our pianist is a woman from the Brazilian congregation. This woman's ability has continuously exceeded our expectations and raised our worship experience to new heights. During the course of a given year, the Brazilian praise group will frequently adorn our American worship celebration by performing in both music and song, bringing glory to Christ through unity.

Work-related cooperative programs to maintain the appearance of your church soon become commonplace in a united ministry. The rebuilding and renovation campaign in our church was greatly accelerated through the combined efforts of three congregations. With a united front we repainted in record-breaking time the exterior of all five buildings on our property along with the interior of the main sanctuary. Finding additional space in our church was made easy through the combined efforts of our three congregations when we cleaned out vital space throughout the facility that had become the storage depository for all the unusable items accumulated over the years. These spaces are now functional rooms.

Cooperative ministries that involve church seniors or youth are another facet of sharing that makes a powerful statement about unity in the church to the unbelieving world. Unified social programs that involve food distribution to the indigent or homeless in your community are another way of spreading the gospel.

3

Preparing Your Congregation for the Guest Group

Two months into my pastorate at NPBC, I called for a congregational meeting to discuss our major guest group, the Brazilian church. It was incumbent upon me as the senior pastor to express my view toward our guests in order to set an example and a precedent for the future attitude of our church. My opening remarks to our church said it all: "In the past two months, I have come to *love* the Brazilian people, and we must embrace them as our own."

My statement gave any of our congregants predisposed to negativity no place to go. My vision for NPBC required us to adopt the mind-set that our guest ministries were indeed part of our church—separate entities, yet part of us.

Since that time, I have constantly strived to build on that platform to promote unity. The tone that was set in the initial meeting fixed the standard for subsequent meetings, so when sensitive or controversial matters, such as yielding up additional space for the guest group or allowing them to make building renovations that would seriously inconvenience the host church, were broached, the congregation leaned toward my discernment and decision making. This was accomplished by persuading my church that our guests were not trying to take us over and that by sharing our church facility with them, we would be greatly blessed by the Lord.

Overcoming Objections

In time, opposing voices did speak out. Their contentions were based on past experiences of abuse by the guest congregations. In the minds of several veteran members there were various misuses: sanctuary infringements (conflicts due to scheduling, running overtime on their worship services, etc.); misleading cultural decorations and signs (erecting posters and banners throughout the facility in Portuguese) that gave the impression that the American church was being squeezed out; discourtesy during the American Bible study classes (disruptions in the halls, excessive noise levels). They argued that this condition, and the emergence of new problems, would only worsen as the guest congregation grew. I believed they had valid arguments, but I was determined to overcome any ill will that lingered from the past.

My thinking in redirecting those who were in pain over the past was to bring them once again to the source that heals and encourages (should we not say *commands?*) unity: the Word of God. By drawing from Paul's example of the unity of believers as members of Christ's body, I would be able to allay any of their fears. The text in 1 Corinthians 12 refers to the proper use of the gifts of the Spirit and can certainly be used to support unity in the church.

The body is a unit, though it is made up of many parts; and though all its parts are many, they form one body. So it is with Christ. For we were all baptized by one Spirit into one body—whether Jews or Greeks, slave or free—and we were all given the one Spirit to drink.

verses 12–13

Central to preparing your church for the guest group should be the Word of God. Your church must be responsive to the Word and consider it the final authority for setting policy in your church. This will enable you to bridge any misunderstandings when you

1. Make it clear to your elected church board and the congregation that the relationship between your church and the guest church is to advance the kingdom of God. Your church must view the undertaking as an extension of your mission program.
2. Make it clear to your board and congregation that they need to catch the vision of unity and consider the inclusion of the guest group as the flash point that may very well ignite a revival in their midst—something that can happen when the Holy Spirit is allowed to reign in the church.
3. Make it clear that the embracing of the guest church is not the pastor's pet project, but it is a carefully thought-out plan led by God's Holy Spirit, approved by the elected church board, and endorsed by the majority of the congregation.

This declaration will undergird your church's purpose in sharing your church as well as clarify your position on missions. Positing this policy from the outset will properly prepare your congregation both spiritually and emotionally. They should see it as the right thing to do because it will please the Lord and because it will encourage a sense of brotherhood between the two cultures.

Gain through Loss

If your church is in a prime location and it is a large facility featuring nicely landscaped grounds, a spacious sanctuary, along with numerous buildings that may include a school and a host of other amenities, it is possible that your congregation may have a problem sharing your church. As it is in the private or individual sector, so too is it in the church environment. Resistance to sharing your church may be due to inordinate pride in the church buildings. This age-old problem can be easily overcome with the proper approach.

You, as the pastor, must make it clear to your congregation that the kingdom of God is not concerned with buildings but with people. Unfortunately, the former was the improper focus of the Israelites during the period of Solomon's temple. The resplendent glory of the temple blinded the people into thinking that the temple made their nation inviolable—that they could do whatever they wanted to and God would overlook it because of the temple. But history shows they were wrong. The lesson is clear: The church building is nothing without God's people, because God's people *are* the church. Your church must remain focused on people.

If indeed God is behind your plan to embrace a guest congregation through a measure of sacrifice, he will not only prepare the hearts of your people to enable them to be a sharing church, but will shower your church with blessings as well. Christ made this abundantly clear: "And everyone who has left houses or brothers or sisters or father or mother or children or fields for my sake will receive a hundred times as much and will inherit eternal life" (Matt. 19:29). Our worship experience must involve *sacrifice* and *sharing*.

This theme became part of our doxology when the Lord did an extraordinary thing shortly after I became the pastor at NPBC. The American church had been in general decline, and finances were very tight, so tight that when the search committee met with me to advise me that I was their choice for the pastor, they added that my paycheck for my first year would come from a small donation they held in the bank—the budget offerings were insufficient to carry the pastor's salary. After that, hopefully, church growth would sustain me. As far as renovations or improvements to the facility were concerned, there were no funds available.

Seven days later a deacon came to me and said, "I have both good and bad news for you."

I scratched the back of my neck and looked at him suspiciously. "What's the bad news?"

The deacon shook his head slightly and with a wrinkled nose said, "An elderly widow in the church by the name of Mrs. Smith died. She had been sick for several years, and passed on a month ago, a few weeks before you came to the church."

I looked at him inquiringly and asked, "And the good news?"

"Well, she left her house to the church." He bit his lip, then shrugged his shoulders and added, "It's a small bungalow-type home that you might decide to keep or we could sell it."

"She had no family?"

"No, she was the sole family member."

Shortly afterward we went to look at the home, and it was apparent from its age that our church would be better off if we sold it and used the proceeds for our budget and improvement fund. We engaged an independent appraiser who estimated its value at $65,000. Our congregation rejoiced at the news, knowing that we could certainly use the money from the sale for our expenses and the much-needed church repairs.

Three weeks later, as God would have it, I received a phone call and subsequent visit from the executor of Mrs. Smith's estate. He informed me that fifteen years earlier, after the death of her husband, she changed her will and left everything to our church.

Out of curiosity I off-handedly asked, "What *is* the value of Mrs. Smith's estate?"

The executor slowly rustled through several papers and then said, "It's about $280,000."

I gulped and said, "Would you repeat that?"

"Mrs. Smith had numerous CD's and bank accounts, and we estimate her holdings to be about $280,000. That includes the value of the house."

After he left, I went through a period of reflection to praise God for his provision. The lesson to me was very clear. First, the Lord wanted me to say "yes" to the search committee, to take that step in faith and become the pastor. Second, the Lord wanted me to respond properly to the task of sharing *his* church—without the benefit of knowing anything about the inheritance the church was about to receive. The decision had to be strictly one of faith and obedience. Gaining through loss is a principle in the kingdom of God.

Maintaining Identity

You may be confronted with the overbearing size of your guest church, which can intimidate the host congregation. From the perspective of maintaining your individual identity, numerical superiority on the part of your guests will probably pose a problem in sharing your church. While it is true that size does not constitute ownership, your church—and visitors to your church—might think your ministry has sacrificed its identity in the sharing process. This topic will be discussed further in chapter 11.

Board and Congregational Approval

Your church must be of one accord when sharing your buildings with another ministry. By unanimously agreeing on the great things of God, your church will keep the unity of the Spirit when it comes to other differences. This is why your elected board and congregation must unanimously approve before any plans to bring in another group are finalized. When the leadership (composed of an elected board, or deacons) is united with the people, this is God's stamp of approval. Anything less may indicate that the plan is destined for failure.

Avoid Misinterpretation

Diplomacy is needed when bringing the proposal to share your church before the congregation. This is especially crucial when your church is going through transition. Most people are averse to change—it's part of their nature. Sheep become very unsettled when there is a rocky pasture ahead of them. Corporate anxiety often accompanies a change of leadership, a building renovation program, or, in particular, a plan to share your church with another group. Great care must be taken to avoid misinterpretation by sending the wrong message to the host congregation. A message that the pastor is treating the guest group with greater care and priority than his own congregation will crush the spirits of the people of the host church. As their shepherd, the pastor must protect the feelings of his sheep by reassuring them that his flock comes first and the guest group second.

Breaking the Language Barrier

If the group seeking to share your church is English-speaking, a language barrier does not apply; otherwise, the group that is soliciting your church to host them will probably be of a different culture and a different language. While many of the church leaders and members may have been in America for a long time, that does not mean they speak English. Many adult foreigners speak no English, others are very slow to learn English (in comparison to their youth, who attend English-speaking schools and learn quickly), while still others speak only a little English, making it difficult to communicate.

Naturally, out of the pool of guests, there will be some who were raised in America by foreign-born parents and speak very good English. Being bilingual, these are the people you need to seek out to aid in breaking down the language barriers in the sharing of your church.

For a time I carried a Portuguese dictionary in my pocket and constantly referred to it when speaking to members of the Brazilian congregation. I frequently use body language, hand signals, and motions to act out a request or response in order to communicate with our guests. Key phrases, salutations, and commands take a little longer to learn but will come easily through practice. Before long I learned which Brazilians could speak English well and constantly sought those persons out to translate. I found that the youth enjoyed translating for the adults, though oftentimes a word or two would be lost in the translation and the adult would suddenly do something totally different than what was asked of him or her through the interpreter. I always smile during those incidents. Ideally, the guests will enjoy learning English since they intend on staying in a predominately English-speaking land.

4

Preparing Your Facility to Accommodate the Guest Group

Care must be taken to properly apportion the amount of space your guest group will use. When I began my ministry at NPBC, I quickly realized that our guest ministries were occupying more than 50 percent of the serviceable area in our facility—our common area being 25 percent. This left a small percentage of useful area for the host church. Clearly, a change was needed. Our guests were using both the sanctuary and fellowship hall at full capacity 85 percent of the time; 75 percent of the administrative offices and school classrooms were also being used full time by the guests. All of the remaining rooms were in such disrepair they had to be completely renovated before they could be functional. This was an imbalance that needed to be corrected.

At a meeting with our guest pastors we hammered out a solution. Since the agreement with both guest ministries was to be long term, it would be imperative that we proportionately allocate according to both present and future need. Presently, due to their size, their ministries required a greater amount of space than ours, but looking to the future—expecting the Lord to bless us numerically—we would need additional space. Therefore, we restricted the use of one building (our education building that required extensive renovating) by both guest ministries, thereby allowing us future expansion. Other buildings, such as our sanctuary and fellowship hall, remain in common use.

Short-term or Long-term Accommodations

Short-term agreements with guest churches range from one to five years. After five years, a long-term agreement would be more suitable. If you, as the host church, are entering into a short-term agreement with another ministry, in the majority of instances, only minor alterations in the facility will be needed. Whether the agreement is short or long, a written agreement is needed (this is further explained in chapter 8).

Short-term Accommodations

Short-term accommodations are temporary in nature. A partial list of items to consider for discussion would consist of:

1. Sanctuary use: An agreement should be in place, setting the days and time of day that the sanctuary will be made available to the guest congregations. Any restrictions should be agreed on in advance of use.
2. Building and room assignments: Those spaces designated to be used by either the host or guest church, or dedicated to be used solely by your guests.
3. Parking lot: Parking can be a major problem for many churches since limited spaces can limit membership growth. Portable parking lot cones can mark off distinct zones for each congregation to avoid overcrowding by one particular church. Regular attenders should

be willing to sacrifice to accommodate space for visitors (a visitor's first and last impression can be altered by his or her parking lot experience).

4. Kitchen: The terms and arrangements for kitchen use need to be constantly reviewed to maintain proper care of each ministry's use of cabinets, utensils, tables, etc.

5. Keys: Unauthorized duplication of keys can wreak havoc in a church. Only staff and responsible persons should have access to keys.

6. Locking Up: One person per congregation should be assigned to lock up. Usually the custodian or a deacon is responsible.

7. Cleanup: The task of cleanup should not be minimized. This important phase of church ministry must be responsibly undertaken by both the host and guest membership to ensure proper care of the facility.

Long-term Accommodations

Long-term accommodations require much more thought and preparation because they invariably involve short-term arrangements as well as permanent changes. A partial list may include:

1. Insurance: Exercising responsibility by informing your insurance carrier of any proposed changes in your building structure is highly recommended. Revisions in your insurance coverage will probably be required in several forms. Consideration should be given in property, liability, and workmen's compensation protection.

2. Interior renovations: An important factor that impacts church ministry is the state of the church buildings themselves, both inside and outside. Rarely will a guest ministry simply move in without requiring some changes in the physical characteristics of their allotted space. An agreement should be in place that describes any painting restrictions (type, color schemes, etc.), electrical modifications, carpet types, and wall parti-

tions. Changes in the rest rooms to accommodate the guest ministry often involve upgrading to bring the renovation up to local codes (handicap-equipped doorways and toilets in accordance with the Americans with Disabilities Act). If the host church was constructed prior to code revisions, modernization can be expensive (sharing these costs is discussed further in chapter 5).

3. Utilities: New telephone, electric, and water service are often required when a guest ministry moves into renovated quarters. The extent and cost for such must be factored into the agreement.

4. Interior amenities: Floral pieces and sanctuary praise banners may fall into the category of short-term, but their cost and continued use may be of a permanent nature. The guest church may decide to hang multiple banners in the worship area (banners can cost thousands of dollars) that may conflict with the host church's form of worship. Floral pieces may be considered beautiful by the guest ministry but too ostentatious for the host church. These issues need to be decided on in your agreement.

5. Musical equipment: The music ministry is an extremely important part of the worship experience in the church. Since the host or guest church may not have its own musical instruments, the decision to share instruments must be made. Sharing costly musical equipment can be hazardous to the church if not properly supervised, however. Disagreements and blame shifting between host and guest churches can arise over disappearance and/or breakage of delicate instruments. In addition, musical equipment has a tendency to proliferate throughout the worship area and can easily take over the sanctuary. To avoid abuses, a responsible person must be put in charge, and boundaries must be set and observed.

6. Audio and video equipment: The audio and video equipment in our church costs over fifteen thousand dollars. It is generally not profitable for both the host and guest

church to purchase their own equipment; duplicate equipment would be cost-prohibitive while sharing seems to be the prudent move. Appointing a sound director for each congregation has proved to be the way to ward off potential problems regarding audio and video equipment. Wireless microphones, amplifiers, and mixing boards, together with the video camera, projector, screen, and the computer to run any Power-Point presentations, must be carefully controlled by a responsible person.

7. Playground: Your guest group will need to share the church playground. This is an extremely important area with parents. They must know that their children's safety can be assured while they attend church functions. In some instances apparatus and perimeter fencing may need to be upgraded to local code requirements. In other cases, providing additional apparatus to accommodate the increased number of children may be necessary.

Storage Areas

Other areas of concern that require explanation are storage areas and temporary building alterations. Whether your church facility is large or small, storage can be a problem once guest ministries are added. To provide adequate storage, you need to take a survey of your existing space to establish availability. Then church leadership will need to make a concerted effort to determine what outdated or unusable stock and equipment—and junk—should be discarded.

When we first began to reorganize our storage at NPBC, we recruited several members from both the host and guest churches to explore and survey all of the nooks and crannies throughout our facility. We discovered that we had over eighty yards of trash to discard! In several rooms in one building we found three aging pianos that were beyond repair, along with church relics like old flags and pictures that simply took up valuable space. Numerous boxes of financial records that dated back forty years consumed three yards of precious space. Near-empty paint containers and assorted paraphernalia took up another two yards. Furniture dating back to primordial days occupied several rooms. Once these areas were cleared, we were able to properly designate storage areas for each ministry.

Our multicultural ministry (American, Brazilian, and Haitian) operates on a full calendar schedule. This means that our facility is rarely in an idle state for more than two weeks at a time during the course of a year. Frequent church events (public or private) invariably require extra tables and chairs and kitchen items (if outside, tents and umbrellas). If the event is for a special holiday (Christmas, Easter, Passover celebration), decorations for you and your guests will be used and later stored. The amount of required storage space can be enormous. While churches will decide to rent many items, frequency of use will soon demand that they be purchased for economical reasons. This means storage space must be allocated. In particular, at NPBC, we had to appropriate storage space for lawn and garden equipment, paint supplies, janitorial supplies, audio/video equipment, Christmas and other holiday decorations, food distribution ministry inventory, outside signs, welcome station materials, and a host of other items.

Temporary Building Alterations

Early in my ministry at NPBC the Brazilian pastor approached me and asked if his congregation could build a temporary stage to extend the altar and choir section of the sanctuary for their Christmas concert. I asked him to give me a rough idea of what that entailed. Little did I know what we were in store for! Like Mennonites constructing a fellow neighbor's barn, the Brazilian congregation rallied and converged to build a 50- by 15-foot stage extension covered with 3/4 inch plywood, undergirded by a labyrinth of two-by-fours, which was then carpeted. The walls were draped with various Portuguese-lettered banners, then the stage sets were fabricated, followed by multiple stage props. Within forty-eight hours, the sanctuary was totally transformed into a Christmas wonderland! It was a terrific display of talent and ingenuity.

After the holiday, I wondered why I never asked them what they were planning to do with all the materials. Where were they going to store them until next year? Well, their solution was simple: They numbered the pieces, dismantled the construction, then asked me for a place of storage. We surveyed our available space and decided that a section on the second floor above our administrative offices would be ideal for storage for temporary events. This space boasts of twenty-two-foot ceilings, enabling us to stack the staging material on industrial shelving in a confined space.

Fortunately, this system worked for us so well that when the Brazilian pastor asked me about their youth conference for which they were planning to transform our sanctuary into a soccer stadium, complete with all the scenery and amenities, I agreed.

5

Agreeing on Renovations

Doctrinal disputes along with immorality and favoritism in leadership are among the many notorious reasons a church divides. Deciding on the color and pattern of the sanctuary carpet should not be one of them. Yet, this issue—along with other decisions on church renovations—has been known to generate a wave of discontent in the congregation. Agreeing on the color of exterior paint for the building and the landscaping shrubs can also become a controversial project tantamount to the decisions made in the United Nations forum. This ought not to be.

It was determined early in my pastorate at NPBC that extensive building renovations were required. The ministry underwent difficult times in the past and a weak budget prohibited ongoing repairs. Leadership changes added to the dilemma as well as the introduction of guest ministries to the church, which led to the postponement of renovations. So, once I was installed as the new senior pastor, the collective ministries looked to me to lead the project. Then, with clipboard in hand, I surveyed all the work that was needed on the facility. The repairs were so extensive that I had to divide the work into two lists: short and long range. The short-range plan would be accomplished within six months; the long-range plan within two years.

The constitution at NPBC requires congregational consent to any purchase or repair above one thousand dollars. Accordingly, the bulk of renovations required approval by the majority of the membership in our church. In some churches this can become a gigantic obstacle when a faction emerges that disagrees with the proposed expenditures, especially if an untried guest ministry is involved. However, at NPBC, the overall spirit of the people was behind me as the pastor, and therefore the recommendations that were put before them met with overwhelming consent. This was due in part to the attitude I projected to the advisory board: "Our guest congregations should be embraced as brethren and since *they* are willing to financially invest in the needed renovations—to form a 'partnership' with us—so, too, should we since *we* own the buildings." The resolution passed unanimously.

Mutual Agreement

Sitting down and discussing our plan over lunch one day, the Brazilian pastor and I hammered out the terms of our agreement. Any costs for major renovations that pertained to areas of common use would be divided in half. This related to the facility's exterior restorations that included the sanctuary, fellowship hall, and surrounding grounds. Any renovations that were specifically designated for the Brazilian church would be borne entirely by that ministry. This included their administrative and education building that they rent from NPBC (located in the rear of our administrative buildings). In time, this agreement was expanded to include the large outdoor recreation area that the Brazilian church uses solely for its picnic and children's playground.

A mutual agreement by both host and guest church can go a long way in promoting your ministry both outwardly and inwardly. Outwardly, your mutual agreement not only honors God but also makes a spiritual statement of unity to the

unbelieving community. And you can be sure that the senti-
ments of your community are extremely important. If you
don't think so, then watch and see how they react when your
church holds a large function such as a crusade, festival, or
seminar. When your neighbors are detained because of con-
gested traffic outside your building or are annoyed because
of the noise emitted from large crowds during a church picnic, you will quickly learn about their view of your ministry.
Complaint calls to code enforcement officials or police will
most definitely put a damper on your ministry. However, if
the community image of your ministry is one of mutual agreement or unity, their level of tolerance is much greater since
they see the church in a larger setting—a setting based on
camaraderie for the greater good of the community in which
they live.

Inwardly, a mutual agreement promotes ownership. Ownership is vitally important when dealing with guest ministries.
If the guest ministry does not have ownership in your church,
then abuses will occur. It has been proved to me over the years
that the guest ministry will treat your property better when
they make a financial investment in the church buildings.
This, too, will promote unity between the host and guest
church.

Property Management Team

Assuming your guest group is in the long-term category, a
property management committee from both the host and
guest group should be designated to facilitate the terms of any
mutual agreement that involves the building and grounds.
The pastor should only oversee the agreement process once
the property management committee has been designated.
James Berkley writes:

> Since it is impossible for the pastor alone to assure that these
> qualities exist, a property committee works well for these pur-
> poses. Usually this committee is made up of laypersons of the
> church who have interest and appropriate skills in construc-

tion, building trades, or facility management. The church may want to include people who have a flair for the aesthetic appeal of the property as well as those with a general interest in maintaining a clean, effective worship facility.[1]

The property management team should be prepared to perform periodic inspections of the facility and arrange the ongoing repairs both during and after the completion of the renovations. Of necessity, their recommendations for equipment replacement will weigh heavily on the annual budget. Berkley adds, "The duties of a property committee might include establishing guidelines for use and maintenance, ensuring safety and security, overseeing costs and equipment purchases, managing custodial operations, and keeping house indoors and outdoors."[2]

The property management team, along with the church leadership, "have a moral obligation to maintain safe, clean, and secure places of worship and ministry."[3] This would include an awareness of any code or deed restrictions since municipalities are now requiring compliance with safety codes and the courts have been making churches liable when people are injured. It follows that the property management team should investigate the possibility of reduced premiums for property and liability insurance when improvements in safety and security to the facility have been made.

Overseeing Expenditures

Gathering information on the proposed renovations by the property management team can yield cost-effective recommendations on both future projects and regularly scheduled maintenance. Berkley notes the following formula:

> From the facility administration budget, the committee can expect to spend about 36 percent in personnel costs, 27 percent in utility costs, 17 percent in building-maintenance costs, and about 10 percent in insurance costs. The remaining funds in the budget go to purchasing supplies and equipment.[4]

Terms of Agreement

Once our agreement was in place we began to hire contractors. This in itself can be a difficult task once you open your church to competitive bids. Having done this, the terms of our agreement meant that we would divide the cost for the following work:

Interior

1.	Sanctuary carpet (incl. install.)	$25,000
2.	Repl. sanctuary air conditioner	$26,000
3.	Painting of sanctuary	$3,000
4.	Electrical renovations	$3,000
5.	Termite treatment	$3,500
6.	Fellowship hall renovations	$3,000
7.	Fellowship hall air conditioner	$4,200
	Total	$67,700

Exterior

1.	New sod lawn	$9,000
2.	Irrigation system	$10,000
3.	Landscaping/tree removal	$4,000
4.	Courtyard patio #1	$12,000
5.	Courtyard patio #2	$5,000
6.	Exterior painting	$5,000
7.	Roofing repairs	$3,500
8.	New sign	$5,200
9.	Driveway/walkway repaving	$4,300
	Total	$58,000
	Grand total	$125,700

Whatever terms of agreement you decide on for long-term tenants, the agreement should impact all the major renovations that are considered permanent. Expenses to renovate *their* designated spaces for *their* ministry, such as administrative offices, classrooms, fellowship, and playground, should be paid for entirely by the guest ministry. Additionally, any temporary facility expense (modular offices/classrooms, tents, canopies, etc.) should also be paid for entirely by the guest church, since they use them.

Drawing on Membership Talents

Our Brazilian guests at NPBC possess battalions of crafts-men. Artisans with terrific talents emerged to aid in the reno-vation process, which promoted a great surge of brotherhood between the two churches. General contractors, carpenters, masons, landscapers, interior decorators, painters, electricians, audio-visual technicians, computer technicians, and a host of others contributed to the work that was needed at our church.

One day while I was visiting the Brazilian administration office, the county electrical inspector came by to examine the work recently completed by the security alarm company. Unfortunately, at the same time, one of the Brazilians was wiring in several electrical receptacle boxes in the same office. The inspector duly noticed the unlicensed worker and imme-diately called for a halt in the work. Naturally, we were embar-rassed and had a talk with the worker, reminding him that only licensed electricians were qualified to do the wiring. For-tunately, the inspector verbally warned us and did not give us a citation.

While not all renovations can be performed by church members due to construction codes requiring licensed con-tractors, a great deal of the detail work can indeed be per-formed by the membership. Work that could be completed on our facility by unlicensed contractors was carefully assigned to our Brazilian brothers who kindly worked either at a great discount or for the cost of materials only. Volun-teers that offer their time and labors should be used when-ever possible. Be sure to show your gratitude to these wor-thy servants.

The overall spirit of the people at NPBC was one that is depicted in the Book of Nehemiah, in which the faithful ral-lied together to rebuild the wall that surrounded Jerusalem. Similarly, we have found that a good maintenance program that keeps the church and grounds in pleasing condition will attract new visitors and potential members.

6

Guests Are Looking for Practical Answers

Every Sunday morning at 8:00, the set-up crew of the West Broward Church arrived at the local elementary school to prepare for the worship service. Their job was to load, transport, unload, set up, and organize the portable pulpit, sound equipment, Sunday school materials, and hymnbooks. Others would regularly join in to move the folding chairs from storage into the auditorium and set them in order before the congregation arrived for Sunday school. After the worship service, everything was neatly put away. This style of doing church went on for more than three years.

For Pastor Mike (Mike is a pseudonym) of the West Broward Church, the joy of ministering to others as their shepherd along with the preaching of God's Word greatly overpowered the inconvenience of "doing church from the trunk of your car." The people, too, rejoiced that this was simply a start-up ministry with great potential, and that God would lead them someday to their own church building. What *did* trouble Pastor Mike was the one thousand dollar per month rent for the use of a public facility for only three hours per week.[1] Besides, he knew it would be impossible to grow a church with only three hours a week when time was needed for Bible study, fellowship, and children's programs. The fact that there were so few schools available made the rent seem somewhat reasonable, but in his heart, he believed the money could buy him many more hours and greater stability if he found another pastor who was willing to share his church until they were ready to settle down and build their own facility.

Renting Space in a School

There are many missions (and some splinter groups) along with start-up churches that are continuously looking to rent space in local schools.[2] Naturally, by their very nature, public schools are required to make the school available to any and all religious denominations and social organizations—primarily on a first-come, first-served basis. This may severely restrict accessibility for the group. Apart from the accessibility factor, there are other considerations, both positive and negative:

1. Since the church is not responsible for the exterior of the school building, there is no upkeep or maintenance to worry about. This will not be a financial responsibility item to the budget (except in the event of vandalism to the school by the churchgoers).
2. Because there is no work on the building and grounds to contend with, organizing workers for strictly internal chores is a much simpler task.
3. Visitors who may otherwise be intimidated by attending a church building may feel quite at ease in the school-church environment.
4. Renting space in a public school does not promote ownership throughout the congregation. It can be expected that members view the school as a mere place of assembly, not a place of worship.

5. As a weekly tenant in a public school, the church will not stabilize. The membership will see themselves as transients—without a place to call their own—and thus, member enrollment will be hindered.
6. Membership growth may be limited. Visitors may view the ministry with a wait-and-see attitude due to the temporary nature of the church setting.
7. Unless the congregation has a clear vision of where the pastor is leading them, and they are solid in their relationship with the Lord, the financial support, or tithing, will be greatly reduced during the sojourn in a local school. People of faith are still human, and they like to see something tangible, besides rent receipts, for their money. This is why church building programs rely heavily on visual aids (photographs of vacant land, architectural drawings and models of the new building, etc.), so people can formulate a picture and idea of the vision that encourages them to support the work of God.

While it is true that a building is not the church (as we have discussed, the church is the body of believers, independent of any building), the idea of a church sharing a public building to hold worship services diminishes the aura of expectation of coming into the presence of God. The argument that God can visit his people in any place such as a sports stadium during an evangelism crusade or revival service is valid, but these locations are only temporary, and not long-term. People respond differently to God's call during crusades and revival meetings than they do during a scheduled Sunday service.

From a Home Front to a Storefront

As a pastor in a Hebrew-Christian church in New York in the early 1980s, I had the privilege of being the leader of a group that began as a home Bible study and ultimately moved into a storefront in a strip mall. For more than two years our group met in someone's home where we studied the Bible, memorized verses, enjoyed fellowship, and made lasting friendships centered around the Lord. We not only served God together through our Bible studies and activities designed to raise our children in the Lord, but we socialized together as well.

This experience as a start-up group was invaluable in the spiritual lives of the participants because the group was small and we really got to know one another. Often this socializing incorporated inviting friends and guests to join our socials, who in turn expressed interest in attending the Bible studies. In this way, the home Bible study acted as a vital artery to bring in new people to hear the Word of God. Before long, we established our church into one large family of God. The period of time we spent as a home Bible study group enabled us to meet without any financial overhead, but we eventually outgrew the home and needed a common place where we could study and worship together as we looked toward expanding the ministry.

One night at the home Bible study, the director, knowing it was time the group move to its own quarters, asked all the faithful members to take a small piece of paper and write out the amount they could tithe to the Lord each month. Once he tallied up the amounts, he announced to the group that we had committed enough monetary support to pay a young pastor and rent our own storefront. We rejoiced that God put our church together.

The congregation rallied to refurbish the vacant store and convert it into a mission center and church. In time we erected a painted sign and strategically placed provocative tracts and prophetic verses in the windows to stir up the hearts of the passersby. Occasionally a walk-in would visit, but for the most part, the congregation consisted of the original home Bible study group. Over the years, congregational growth remained small. This was the experience of our congregation, and although with other ministries and their relative size, conditions may vary, I believe the general principles still hold.

There are many advantages to renting a storefront, such as (1) public exposure on a main thoroughfare, (2) reduced upkeep on the building (generally, the landlord takes care of the exterior of the building), (3) lower operating costs (normally, rent plus utilities), (4) mobility (if the location does not work out, you can move before renewing the lease). In my opinion, however, numerical growth in the storefront was restricted for these reasons:

1. By virtue of association with the other commercial enterprises in the mall, the image of the church in the community seemed to fall into the category of a business, not a ministry. The community could not separate the church from the rest of the stores in the mall. They viewed the church as another merchandising vendor in the shopping district. It was difficult to elevate the prestige of the church in the community.
2. The neighborhood environment was not conducive for a church. There needs to be a certain reverence for church property, and while there was adequate exposure to the public, the public mistreated the storefront by abusive parking, uncontrollable litter, and general disregard for church possessions.

Circumstances that contribute to the lack of growth in a home Bible study group or a storefront ministry may vary, but overall, I see that station in the life of a church as being only temporary, because a healthy church should eventually take the step of faith and seek a building of its own. Rick Warren in *The Purpose-Driven Church* writes, "If you're not taking risks in your ministry, then it is not requiring that you have faith. And if your ministry doesn't require any faith, then you are being unfaithful."[3] However, until the group is ready to begin a building program, sharing a church with another congregation may be more practical.

Practical Considerations

The Right Time to Move into a Church

As a general rule, a group should not attempt to move into a church to share its facility until they are able to meet their own future operating expenses. These operating expenses should include the pastor's salary (full or part time). While in a home Bible study atmosphere, the group generally remains relatively small, but when the core group is of an appreciable size (probably around fifty in number), that is an indicator that the time has come to move into larger quarters. This size group may consider shopping for an established host church.

The group in the fifty-plus range should not overtax the host church. Yet, this size group is large enough to engage in the activities necessary to push the enrollment to over two hundred. Once the guest group grows to more than two hundred, the leadership should consider constructing their own building and making preparations to relocate.

A Friendly Environment

The pastor of a guest church will be concerned with the cultural condition of the community and the geographic location of the host church. Naturally, an ethnically different guest group would be concerned if the host church was located in a community where racial bias is a problem. It is not too difficult to imagine that an African American group looking to share a church in a predominately white neighborhood that is opposed to integration could pose some difficulties. From my experience of over fifteen years in a Hebrew-Christian ministry, I know that sensitivity to the community in which you plant your church makes all the difference in winning people to Christ. The guest pastor should look for a church in a neighborhood that will not be offended by their presence, which in turn will impact their effectiveness.

A pastor friend of mine who was searching for a host church came upon a church that offered great potential for his group. The facility was large, so it could easily accommodate the group, and the rent was very reasonable. But the condition of the community surrounding the host church appeared hostile and undesirable, and he believed it would hinder the growth of his ministry. A friendly environment is crucial in the life of both the host and guest groups.

A Church That Offers a Good Example

The aphorism "No one is more confusing than someone who gives advice while setting a bad example" is a general principle that applies to a host church as well as to individuals. The guest group needs the host church to act as a positive influence. It is to be expected that the guest church will view the host church as a model church in action. Just as young believers in a church lean on mature believers for guidance, so too does the guest group look to learn from the mature believers in the host group. Observers from the guest church will be vigilant to see how their landlord "does church." A good example will promote a rapport between host and guest and will give the guests legitimacy of purpose.

An Opportunity to Save Money

There are many fledgling groups that cannot survive unless they receive assistance from an established ministry. Renting space in an established church is rapidly becoming a viable alternative for missions and start-up churches who want to begin financial structuring that will lead to building their own church.

Commercial landlords do not consider the financial needs or goals of a group looking to rent a building for a church. Accordingly, renting space in the secular world will cost your church a considerable amount more than if you share with another church. Likewise, commercial landlords are not bound by any biblical injunction to help those looking for their own quarters to set up church. But the Christian pastor *is* obliged to consider the financial needs and biblical principles that demand deference to a needy sister ministry.

Having established this platform, the guest pastor looking to share a church should keep in mind that sharing a church will result in greatly reduced operating expenses, which will enable the guest church to save money. In the case of the Brazilian ministry that shares our church, in five years they have saved enough money to begin building their own facility.

A Chance to Enhance Stability

After the covenants are in place and the deal to share a church has been consummated, the guest group will look to settle into its normal routines of church life as soon as possible. This important step in relocation enhances its stability in the host church as well as promoting stability within its own congregation. Stability is crucial, because the sooner the congregation is planted, the sooner it will grow and blossom.

The normal routine must allow for the use of the sanctuary for the fundamentals of church life, including weddings, funerals, and holiday productions. The guest pastor may also see whether there is a fellowship hall for receptions, luncheons, dinners, and general meetings.

Another area of concern that engenders stability between host and guest is the potential for expansion. This sharing of resources by the host church must include room for future expansion of the guest ministry. Every guest ministry dreams of growing, and with that ambition comes the need for additional space. The potential for the guest church's future expansion will impact your candidacy for being a host church.

7

Guests Are Looking for Scriptural Answers

After speaking with the Brazilian pastor about his life in South America before he immigrated to the United States, I tried to visualize what it would be like to be a foreigner in a strange land. Like myself, most Americans are native-born, and few can relate to the trauma of being transplanted several thousand miles from their birthplace and beginning a new life. It truly is a hard thing. This is why God warned the Israelites to extend a special form of protection and blessing to the foreigner: "Do not mistreat an alien or oppress him, for you were aliens in Egypt" (Exod. 22:21).

The Hebrew word for alien is *geyr*, which is properly a *guest* or, by implication, a *foreigner*. We can also substitute the word *stranger*. A *foreigner* is defined as "A person from a different racial, ethnic, and linguistic group as in contrast to a 'native.'"[1] To appreciate what your guests (or "aliens") are looking for in your church, it is instructive to delve into Old Testament history.

The Foreigner in the Old Testament

We read in Genesis that after the fall of man in Eden, all of humanity through Adam is exiled from God's presence and banished to a foreign land. With this backdrop we can readily see how a migrating settler became known as a stranger, a temporary resident, or more generally, an outsider, excluded from the native race, tribe, or family. In time, the fall gave rise to a "divided humanity, alienated from God and from itself . . . in desperate need of a home."[2] This ocean of humanity became many nations before Abraham (who received a divine decree to leave his pagan land of Mesopotamia to become a resident alien in Canaan), who was the father of many nations as well as the progenitor of the nation of Israel. Through this pilgrim migration came the Abrahamic promise that would designate Israel as the Promised Land for the Hebrews, while their existence would be dedicated to being a blessing to foreigners (Gen. 12:3). So "when Israel was constituted as a nation at Sinai (Exodus 19–24), a concern for resident aliens was etched into the legal system."[3]

Israel, then, by experience and necessity, was unique in their regard for the alien:

> The alien peoples received special protection under the law (Exod. 22:21; 23:9), and were even to be loved as native Israelites (Lev. 19:34). Such protection was particularly necessary as immigrants would not have the social network of kinship relations for support during exigencies. Yet, although ancient Near Eastern law codes stressed protection for the widow and orphan, only Israel's contained legislation for the resident alien. This was probably due to the peculiar circumstances of her origin.[4]

During the kingdom period, Solomon instructed his people that the temple would be a house of prayer for all peoples, as Israelites and "aliens" could pray to the Lord (1 Kings 8:41–43; Isa. 56:3–8). In Isaiah (2:1–4) and Micah (4:1–5), the Scriptures foretold that all nations would go to Jerusalem to be instructed in the ways of the Lord and no longer be polarized from each other. Parenthetically speaking, Israel itself would be reminded that the land it would possess belonged to God and that he allowed the Israelites to settle on it as resident aliens awaiting their permanent place as the head of all nations during the messianic period, the millennium.

The Foreigner in the New Testament

We find in the Old Testament that God's design for evangelizing the surrounding nations was to draw them to the land of Israel through various means. Israel will always be central to God's plan. The very oracles of God were committed to the Jewish people (Exod. 19:4–6; Ps. 147:19–20; Rom. 3:2). In addition, they had the voice of the prophets as well as the holy priesthood; and, of course, they had the temple, along with all of the hallowed artifacts that accompanied it. Through these evangelistic means, the Lord was declaring his missionary call to the foreigner: "Come!"

But with the Great Commission (Matt. 28:19–20), everything changed. The Lord decreed a new form of evangelizing the foreigner. With a thunderous boom he declared to the church, "Go!" Christ's teaching made it clear that the new covenant not only instructed the church to go out from its land—its comfort zone—to reach the foreigner, but also taught that God's love now embraced the whole world. "Meanwhile the church must act by helping literal strangers and foreigners, remembering her own identity and God's love for the powerless (Matt. 25:35, 38, 43, 44)."[5] Allegorically, the author of Hebrews, citing Abraham's journey, declared:

> By faith Abraham, when called to go to a place he would later receive as his inheritance, obeyed and went, even though he did not know where he was going. By faith he made his home in the promised land like a stranger in a foreign country; he lived in tents, as did Isaac and Jacob, who were heirs with him of the same promise. For he was looking forward to the city with foundations, whose architect and builder is God.
>
> Hebrews 11:8–10

Paul reiterated the view taught in Hebrews when he announced:

> Remember that at that time you [the Gentiles] were separate from Christ, excluded from citizenship in Israel and foreigners to the covenants of the promise, without hope and without God in the world. But now in Christ Jesus you who once were far away have been brought near through the blood of Christ.
>
> Ephesians 2:12–13

This served as a reminder that the Gentile foreigner would now be embraced by the God of Israel. The church lives like the stranger, similar to the pilgrim—simply resident aliens on earth, analogous to Abraham—before they receive their permanent citizenship in heaven (1 Peter 1:17; 2:11).

Apparently foreigners are looking for a home away from home, a place where they will be warmly received despite their alien status. God expects his church to have a love for the stranger, namely by showing hospitality (*philozenos* in Greek) that is expressed as a characteristic of the believer (1 Peter 4:9; Rom. 12:13).

Your Guests Want to Promote
the Christian Testimony

Most guest ministries are very grateful to your church for allowing them to share your facility. And you can be sure your guest ministry is very concerned about its image in the community. The Brazilian pastor at my church constantly questions me about the neighborhood's response to their presence. They want to be liked by people in America, the country for which they left their home. They don't want to intrude or displace; they simply want to impact for Christ in their own culture and live out their lives as best they can in the "land of opportunity." Therefore, a unified testimony between the

American and guest groups represents an important part of their goal to settle in a foreign land.

When the host and guest ministries bond together in unity, this represents a common witness to the community that cannot be denied. In other words, the neighboring community sees that the host American church has extended itself to embrace the foreigner, which is going to heighten the level of acceptance for the foreigner in the community. Naturally, the guest church would be looking to raise this level of acceptance in the region.

Jesus had the goal of using unity to promote the Christian church when he prayed,

> "My prayer is not for them [his disciples] alone. I pray also for those who will believe in me through their message, that *all of them may be one,* Father, just as you are in me and I am in you. May they also be in us so that the world may believe that you have sent me. I have given them the glory that you gave me, *that they may be one as we are one."*
>
> John 17:20–22, italics mine

Your Guests Are Looking for Empathy

The case of Vava (a nickname) is very interesting. His real name is Rivaldo Santos, and he is a forty-year-old Brazilian immigrant who came to our Brazilian ministry in 1999. Vava sadly, yet purposely, left his wife Rozenilda and their four young boys back in Brazil for more than a year so he could earn enough money to bring them to America. Possessing only his faith in Christ, a powerful resolve, and brute strength, he took on the mammoth task of being the custodian for our entire facility. Considering he couldn't speak a word of English and that he was detached from his family with no place to call home (he simply bunked in with other Brazilians), this man performed like a workhorse, determined to reunite his family on the shores of South Florida. Vava now enjoys the company of his entire family who, together, perform their service to the Lord by taking care of our buildings. It was through this man that I began to empathize with the plight of the foreigner. I came to realize that Christ's church is for all who will come into it; thus, there are no longer any special qualifications, like nationality. Further, I came to realize that empathy is one of the reasons why the Brazilian church is as successful as it is; they all empathize with each other. It is understandable, then, that they would look to see a spirit of empathy from their host church.

This empathy is one of the key characters in genuine fellowship. It embraces the thought that we would share, vicariously, the conflict that accompanies foreigners until they are resettled. As Millard Erickson relates,

> This does not mean merely a social interrelatedness, but an intimate feeling for and understanding of one another. There are to be empathy and encouragement (edification). What is experienced by one is to be experienced by all. Thus Paul writes, "If one member suffers, all suffer together; if one member is honored, all rejoice together" (1 Cor. 12:26).[6]

Your Guests Yearn for Unity of Spirit

Bringing in groups of the same denomination to share your church is very important to the integrity and welfare of your ministry. Bringing in groups with the same spirit is equally important. In the case of NPBC, the three pastors are all of the same heart and spirit. This is not uniformity, but unity. We have a oneness in vision and purpose that was exemplified by the early church, where, we find in Acts 4:32, "All believers were one in heart and mind."

This narrative in Acts is not for the purpose of providing us with an academic study of early church history but is designed to set an example for future church life. Beginning with the leadership and trickling down into the congregation, the message is clear: We must be united in both heart

---

Union has an affiliation with others but no common bond that makes them one in heart. *Uniformity* has everyone looking and thinking alike. *Unanimity* is complete agreement across the board. *Unity*, however, refers to a oneness of heart, a similarity of purpose, and an agreement on major points of doctrine.
—Charles R. Swindoll, *The Tale of the Tardy Oxcart*[7]

---

and mind—and the Spirit—thereby making us eligible to receive God's richest blessings.

In practicality, maintaining unity in the Spirit despite our divergent ministries requires a higher form of sharing: sharing possessions. This is one of the supreme tests of spiritual unity, as is depicted, once again, in the early church, where "All the believers were together and had everything in common. . . . No one claimed that any of his possessions was his own, but they shared everything they had" (Acts 2:44; 4:32).

Because our Brazilian guests are grateful to God for the opportunity of sharing our church, they are very eager to share their material possessions with us. This is a living testimony of the yearning for unity of spirit. In our case, the Brazilian ministry is much larger than the American ministry, and its financial resources are greater by proportion. This means that they are able to afford new and better things, from music and audio/visual equipment to holding conferences with Brazilian celebrities.

Because they yearn for unity of spirit, they are the first to share all they have. It is never a question of "yours" and "mine," but "ours."

Your Guests Want Growth

Your guest ministry is certainly interested in growth. Most mission churches begin with a meager core group that anticipates future development to a constitutionalized church status. When there is unity with the host church as well as internally in their own ranks, their testimony and propensity for growth is greatly enhanced. Millard Erickson writes,

> The company of believers tends to grow when their witness is united, whereas there may well be a negative or canceling effect when they compete with or even criticize one another. Certainly the gospel witness is not reinforced by the existence of competitive groups.[8]

Conversely, a lack of unity not only retards growth in both the host and guest church, but it actually means a reduplication of efforts. Your guest group will of necessity be diligent to survey and learn of any efforts on the part of the host church to minimize the wasting of their precious and restricted resources, whether it be in money, material, or personnel. Consequently, they will note the host church's willingness to share their resources with them.

Your Guests Want Good Relationships

Your guest leaders are not looking for a good landlord-tenant relationship with the host church. That kind of an alliance is available in the secular world. No, they are looking for a landlord-tenant relationship that has spiritual "teeth" in it. A good relationship with spiritual teeth is one that enables the leadership to deal with weighty, and sometimes thorny, issues and still walk away from the discussion table praising the Lord for each other. This kind of a relationship must be effusive at the top before it can filter down into the pew. This kind of spiritual relationship will set the standard for the atmosphere throughout the congregations. Naturally, this requires the pastor-to-pastor association to be of the highest caliber.

The Brazilian pastor and I discussed the issue of relationships in the beginning stages of our affiliation, bringing up the operative words *mutual respect,* which would become a fundamental element in our ministry credo. This is very important because, invariably, disputes and disagreements between sharing congregations occur within the church. If they are not handled properly, they become thorny issues. When a difficult situation arises between me and a member of the Brazilian church, our mutual-respect agreement does not allow me as the senior pastor to reprimand or scold a member of the Brazilian church. The dispute is simply taken up with my fellow pastor at our weekly luncheon, or if it is urgent, by phone; he then takes care of it. This ensures a good relationship.

Your Guests Look for the Host Church to Be Teachable

Sharing your church will involve cultural differences that can easily become a point of contention between the two ministries. This is the reason the host church must be teachable. By teachable I mean that they are able to be instructed or flexible when it comes to understanding the customs, manners, and even the scheduling of the divergent culture that has come to the church.

The congregation at NPBC is mostly traditional as opposed to contemporary. While this has its blessings when it comes to worship music, the Brazilian church is totally the opposite—ultracontemporary. Their musical instruments consist of Spanish and electric guitars, electronic keyboards, a complete set of drums, and a piano. Their style of singing is far from the sound American ears are accustomed to.

In one instance, the Brazilian music minister petitioned me to permanently spread their instruments all over our raised platform altar area. This would mean the removal of all the choir chairs, the modesty rail, and any other traditional items to make a place for the instruments. Initially I made some concessions to remove the chairs and modesty rail, stipulating that they confine their instruments to a small corner of the altar area. If they had to spread them out during worship, they were required to return them to the corner after use. We operated in this fashion for several months, but all the while I realized that the Brazilian ministry cooperated under duress.

One day I visited their Sunday service and became so overwhelmed by their praise and worship time that my heart capitulated. God's Spirit impressed upon me the truth that I had to be teachable. Soon afterward I met with their worship leader and gave my permission to fully extend their instruments throughout the altar area. The Brazilian pastor later told me in confidence that two months down the line the music minister began to cast her eye toward the organ that stood opposite the piano. She began to think how good their drums would sound from that location. But when I reminded him that our veteran members viewed the organ as the last vestige of their traditional worship, he quickly dismissed the notion.

Services conducted by the guest church may constitute schedule variances that conflict with the host church. Being teachable means making adjustments to accommodate the guests. In our case at NPBC, the Brazilian church has a heavy evening schedule; they operate some aspect of their ministry nearly every night. Ordinarily, this would constitute a schedule conflict, but we became teachable (pliable, if you will), allowing them to use our sanctuary while we used adjacent rooms.

We are determined not to allow any obstacle to come between us. As Paul puts it, "For I resolved to know nothing while I was with you except Jesus Christ and him crucified" (1 Cor. 2:2).

8

Is Shaking Hands Enough?

Oral communication between two persons who speak different languages can present quite a problem when attempting to establish agreements, even if they shake on it. While universal body gestures and hand motions may aid in reducing lingual barriers at the point of contact, invariably some of the message gets lost in the translation. In the passage of time, a great deal of the verbal message can become fuzzy, distorted, or downright unclear.

While the shaking of hands in this context can mean "welcome," or "let's come to an understanding," or even "let's make a mutual agreement," the fact is it represents a poor means of establishing an agreement in our society today. Someone could argue that in the secular world the act of simply shaking hands to consummate an agreement could pose a serious threat to business by creating gross misunderstandings that could cause financial loss or generate fraudulent claims. Therefore, there must be *written* agreements to protect the two parties. But is there a need to formulate a written agreement in the church? After all, we have a common bond in

Jesus, so isn't shaking hands enough? The answer to the question is a resounding No!

Years ago this problem became apparent to the leadership at NPBC when couples would ask to rent our sanctuary for their wedding ceremony. In those early years a handshake was satisfactory to consummate the agreement. But in time, because of abuses and struggles, the church required a written document to avoid any further problems—the handshake was no longer a viable means of protecting the church. Later, when we began sharing our church with the Brazilians, our wedding agreement that had instructed the English-speaking people on conditions, policies, and deposits was no longer adequate, because many words in English do not properly translate to Portuguese. We often encountered difficulties due to language barriers, so, to avoid any misunderstandings, we agreed on a rental covenant (revised and clarified with the help of the Brazilian leadership) to protect our future relationship. This minor problem set the standard for other functions such as bridal showers and receptions, birthday and anniversary parties.

Written Covenants Promote Unity

The covenant dates back to antiquity, where we find that the ancient Assyrians entered into what was called the *biritu* (*berith* in Hebrew), which has the common meaning "fetter," but also means "covenant." It is probable that this led to the meaning "to bind," but this is not certain. If indeed the root word is "to bind," then the covenant is designed to bind together the parties. In the Old Testament, the term has a twofold meaning: In a religious sense, it denotes a solemn agreement between God and man, or in a general use, a binding contract or pledge between two men.

In the ancient Arab culture, this tribal covenant was binding in a brotherhood by the drinking of each other's blood. Later modifications in the ancient practice brought the drinking of sacrificial blood, or the sprinkling of it on the people involved. In time, the usage took on the form of eating together the sacrificial meal (Gen. 26:25–31). Sometimes the word *oath* is used as the equivalent, where God is called in as a witness. Biblically speaking, the majority of covenants take place between larger groups beginning with the kings and continuing down to the tribes or clans. The breaking of the covenant was regarded as a serious sin.

Today we have the written covenant from God in the form of the Bible. The Bible clearly spells out the agreement between God and man and how we are reconciled to him through Christ, along with the agreement necessary to promote a proper relationship among human beings. God has established the need for written covenants to maintain the proper communication and unity between both parties: those in heaven and those on the earth.

The Operations Covenant

After two years of our daily routine at NPBC, I noticed a mood change coming over many of the members of the American congregation. It took the form of a general malaise that threatened to spread and bring injury to our church. Leadership discussions together with questioning the congregation brought me to the conclusion that many of our members were feeling intimidated by the relentless quest for more space by our Brazilian guests. Their church was expanding at such a rapid rate that any room on the premises was targeted for their use, despite my continued refusal. My refusal was based on this reason: "NPBC cannot yield up any additional space without compromising the integrity of our ministry's future expansion."[1] Additionally, there were violations in Christian courtesy as well as unauthorized renovations. This brought us to the place where we needed an Operations Covenant.

As Ralph Wilson observes,

> Beyond an initial statement of Christian convictions, both the host and guest congregations need to understand clearly from

the beginning the privileges and responsibilities that go with
sharing. For this purpose a written covenant or agreement
should be prepared in the languages of both congregations.[2]

The Operations Covenant was designed to keep misunderstandings to a minimum. We were acting together in a
united way as Christian brothers and sisters, but because of
cultural differences and their mammoth size, we were losing
our unity. Stig Hanson concurs with this position in his argument in favor of unity:

> Because God is one, the people of Israel were expected to wor-
> ship him with all their heart. Moreover, because God is one,
> the universe is truly one. All of it has been created by God, as
> Genesis 1 teaches; the entire world, being a unity, conforms
> to the will of its Creator. Since everything, including man, has
> a common origin and one Lord, it is altogether fitting, indeed
> it is imperative, that believers unite.[3]

Again, to promote unity, I resolved to establish clear parameters in writing. Having a covenant between the host and
guest church is similar to referring to a handbook when a difficulty arises. Whether it be for military, governmental, corporate, or commercial use, the handbook represents an
invaluable tool to settle disputes by affirming and redefining
predetermined agreements. We draw from James Berkley's
advice:

> Policies are management decisions that express a church's
> operating philosophy. Policies answer questions before they
> are asked and guide people in responding to routine situa-
> tions before problems occur. Every church should develop
> policies that convey the desires of its members. The policies
> should be formulated in concert with those who will imple-
> ment them, according to stated procedures.

> Policies are best communicated in writing. When voted on by
> the congregation, they become a permanent expression of the
> church's mission and purpose. They also serve as a manual of
> training for new staff and committee members, a guide for

making future decisions, and a handbook of church operations for the membership. . . . Churches should strive to transmit policies in standard ways, since the reason for policies is to encourage consistent administration.[4]

The fundamental reason for the Operations Covenant is to cool down conflicts and minimize difficulties. Without question, a clear agreement will protect continued harmony between the host and guest ministries. This, of necessity, requires that each item be clearly detailed.

Model Operations Covenant

As previously mentioned, short-term agreements with guest churches range from one to five years. After five years, a long-term agreement would be more suitable. In either case, a written covenant is recommended. The covenant should include the following items:[5]

1. Complete name and address of the guest ministry, names of pastors and leaders, and at least two emergency contact telephone numbers.
2. The dates for which the agreement is effective.
3. An initial list of rooms to be used and times of use, which may be changed by mutual agreement.
4. Kitchen arrangements: designated cabinets, utensils, pots, etc. Items to be shared: tables, refrigerators, stoves, coffeepots, etc. Clean-up policy.
5. Use of audio-visual and computer equipment (see chapter 4 for details).
6. Parking lot restrictions.
7. Cleaning arrangements. How much is expected of the guest group? What is the custodian's responsibility? Responsibility for setting up, moving, and putting away chairs and tables.
8. Agreement on child supervision.
9. Designated person to lock up; key distribution and control.

10. Agreement on the sign (refer to chapter 10).
11. Facility workday participation guidelines.
12. Financial responsibilities for damages.
13. Insurance (property and liability) agreement. Separate or collective policies?
14. The amount of shared expenses to be charged if any (details on this subject are covered in the next section).
15. Leadership change provision.
16. A procedure to terminate the relationship, if that becomes necessary. Time to relocate to another facility (60–90 days with a warm farewell).
17. The final agreement should be signed by all the leaders of all congregations.

The Covenant: A Basis of Authority

The Operations Covenant should be treated as the constitution between the host and guest churches. This is apart from the church's own constitution formulated by the founding fathers of the church denomination. In the arena of the church, Christian counseling, and Christian academia, we have the Bible as the basis of our authority, with commentaries and the philosophies of men trailing behind. Comparatively, when we look to the court of law and the legal profession, they have both the U.S. Constitution and case law as the basis of their authority when deciding verdicts and rulings.

From this covenant between host and guest churches should emerge clear parameters that define both the privileges and responsibilities of sharing. The regular periodic review of the Operations Covenant should encourage ongoing communication and open dialogue in the leadership and work its way down to the membership. When the Operations Covenant serves as the guideline for church procedure and behavior, it will eliminate the need for constant surveillance on the part of the host church.

Before the Operations Covenant was in place at NPBC, any violation of Christian courtesy or protocol on the part of the guest group became a point of contention that seemed to snowball into a serious matter within forty-eight hours. Unfortunately, several minor offenses would be stacked up by the "observer" until a large pile formed. This pile would then be placed at the pastor's door so that he would fall over it as he left his office on the way to lunch. It would then be the pastor's task to take care of the violation. With the advent of the Operations Covenant that provided guidelines detailing what is expected between the host and guest ministries, a great deal of this unnecessary watchdog mentality has been disposed of.

The Shared Expense Covenant

Surprisingly, when I became the pastor of NPBC I learned that the guest ministries were actually costing us money. While *they* were flourishing, the NPBC host church was bordering on returning to mission status because of lack of financial support. The cost of the utilities and maintenance for the facility was greater than the rental income we were receiving from the guest ministries. This was one of the reasons why we instituted the Shared Expense Covenant.[6]

Other reasons also prevailed upon us. Namely, the Shared Expense Covenant is a document, a tangible agreement that endorses good financial stewardship and lessens the financial burden of the host church. In addition, the Shared Expense Covenant promotes a feeling of ownership of the entire facility, which encourages better treatment of the facility. These are the fundamental reasons why guest churches should not be allowed to occupy your facility rent free. It is also incumbent on the host church that the rent agreement and the Shared Expense Covenant bring in an income that exceeds the operating expenses. Any church leadership that allows a guest ministry to occupy its facility just to cover expenses is exposing itself to criticism from the congregation. In time, the host church membership will resent the sacrifices: the overcrowding, the wear and tear on the building and furnishings, the kitchen abuses, the conflict in schedules, and the various and sundry nuisances that accompany sharing a church. There needs to be some compensation coming back to the host church to offset these elements that promote dissatisfaction between the groups. In addition, and perhaps more importantly, there is no theological or biblical reason why the host church should not be entitled to benefit from sharing their church building.

If, indeed, the guest church is a start-up ministry or a struggling church that is operating on a shoestring budget in which its tithes, offerings, and other support are rather meager, then the host church should require a board approval or congregational vote to take the guests in as a mission. The decision as to whether the host church should require from the mission church fair and reasonable rent, as well as paying its portion toward the Shared Expense Covenant as opposed to merely paying a small contribution as a sign of good faith, should rest with the elected board and congregation.[7] If the host church's heart attitude is one of sacrifice to enable the fledgling church to get off the ground, then the leadership must view it as coming from the mind of the Lord.

Types of Covenant

1. Step-Up Covenant: This kind of arrangement works well with the guest church that is either a start-up or struggling ministry. Both the rent and the Shared Expense Covenant start out at a specified amount that is considerably lower than the prime rate, and then on a specified future date(s), the rate increases or steps up. There may be graduated rate hikes over a few years that enable the guest church an opportunity to build up their congregation.
2. Percentage Covenant: Another covenant that may be suitable is the percentage formula. This uses a given percentage of the guest church's annual budget as the mean that determines the amount of either the rent or

Shared Expense Covenant (or both). If the annual budget of the guest ministry is $30,000, then a modest amount of 10 percent or $3,000 would be its annual rent. Its proportionate contribution toward the Shared Expense Covenant would be 10 percent of the agreed expenditures or expenses.

3. Proportionate Use Covenant: The amount of rent and the percentage of shared expenses is determined by the volume of space the guest church purposes to occupy. When the guest ministry occupies 40 percent of the facility, its rent would be equivalent to 40 percent of the host church's mortgage payment. If the guest ministry uses the facility 70 percent of the time, then its shared expenses would be 70 percent.

4. Proportionate/Split Covenant: The amount of rent is determined by the volume of space the guest church purposes to occupy (above), while the shared expenses are divided equally.

5. Split-Expense Covenant: Simply put, this form of covenant divides all expenses in half between the host and guest ministry. The mortgage payment along with all the utilities, capital expenditures, maintenance, and renovations are divided equally.

6. Standard/Split-Expense Covenant: This is a common form of covenant where the rent includes all utilities, but any capital improvement expenses (e.g., replacing the air-conditioning system, the septic tank, the electrical system, the roof) would be split between the host and guest churches.

7. Frequency of Use Covenant: Another common, but not necessarily equitable to the host church, form of covenant is the Frequency of Use Covenant. With this type of arrangement the host church charges the guest ministry each time it uses the facility. Some of the problems that are often encountered with this form are wear and tear, inconvenience, escalating expenses (e.g., utility rate increases during heating/cooling seasons).

Model Shared Expense Covenant[8]

Fixed Expenses
1. Mortgage	Host church includes in guest rental
2. Utilities:	
a. Electric	70 percent
b. Water	50 percent
c. Garbage	50 percent
d. Telephone	Guest ministry expense
3. Custodian	50 percent
4. Insurance (liab. & prop.)	Proportionate[9]

Capital Improvements
1. Common areas[10]	50 percent
2. Guest occupied areas[11]	Guest ministry expense
3. Designated areas[12]	Split, proportionate, or guest ministry expense

Maintenance
1. Common areas	50 percent
2. Guest occupied areas	Split, proportionate, or guest ministry expense
3. Designated areas	Guest ministry expense

These prototype models can be adapted to fit the individual needs of each church.

It's the Spirit That Counts

The most important and fundamental principle that must be observed in dealing with guest ministries when it comes to the buildings is that the host church should never become a "facility manager" for the guests. The buildings and the operation thereof should always be subordinate to the fruit of the Spirit. As Samuel Chadwick so aptly puts it:

> God cares nothing for costly buildings, and everything for loving hearts. He seeks men. He wants men. He needs men. He dwells in men. . . . Men are God's method. The Church is looking for better methods; God is looking for better men. He has staked His kingdom on men. He has trusted His Gospel to men. He has given His Spirit to men. The Church is on the stretch for new methods, new plans, new buildings,

new organizations, but "the eyes of the Lord go to and from throughout the earth, to show Himself strong in the behalf of them whose heart is perfect/mature toward Him." The Holy Spirit does not come upon methods, but upon men. He does not anoint machinery, but men. He does not work through organizations, but through men. He indwells the Body of Christ, directs its activities, distributes its forces, empowers its members.[13]

9

Setting Boundaries to Minimize Conflicts

Early one Sunday morning, the ladies of the NPBC were in the kitchen of our fellowship hall preparing for our monthly luncheon when suddenly they realized the cooking and eating utensils were missing. A fiery contingent immediately brought proceedings against our Brazilian ministry for taking them, then summoned the pastor to execute judgment. They may have expected instant justice, but I delayed execution until we spoke with the Brazilian hostess. We soon learned that the utensils were accidentally misplaced (not intentionally as some assumed), and the mini-melee subsided. The incident, however, did bring to mind that little things can quickly escalate into big things unless boundaries are in place to avoid conflicts.

Spirit of Peacemaking

Despite the agreement cited in the model Operations Covenant defining the kitchen procedure, occasional disputes do happen. This is why it is vitally important that there be a

Conflicting expectations are like a tight shoe. They begin with a pinch, but if left unattended, they soon become painfully tender to the slightest touch.

—Richard P. Hansen, *Leadership,* vol. 5, no. 3

spirit of peacemaking between congregations. As John Trapp said, "The devil loves to fish in troubled waters."

Christ pronounced his blessing on the peacemaker (Matt. 5:9), and Paul builds on that premise by encouraging unity in the body of Christ through peacemaking: "Make every effort to keep the unity of the Spirit through the bond of peace" (Eph. 4:3). In addition to having clarity and understanding about the covenant and its parameters, the spirit of peacemaking will help govern the attitude of the people and raise their level of tolerance, which will minimize conflict.

This spirit of peacemaking has taken up residence in the leadership at NPBC, thereby allowing us the freedom to concentrate on weightier issues. During our weekly luncheons, the Brazilian pastor and I discuss what I call "nuisance issues." This is in addition to the weightier issues, those significant discussions that radically affect the direction of our ministry. These nuisance issues are not grave enough to fight over, but small enough to discuss (to minimize future conflicts).

Examples of typical nuisance issues we discuss are recurrent clutter involving the musical instruments on the sanctuary stage, snack food/containers left in the sanctuary in violation of the "No Food or Drink" order, stains on the carpet, bubble gum compressed into the concrete on the walkways, excessive litter, both inside and outside the facility, and discourtesy between the members of the congregation and/or the leadership. Each one of us notes these items on our memo pads after our lunch, ensuring they will be duly handled in an expedient fashion. Experience in promptly handling these items has significantly reduced the level of conflict between congregations.

Hands-on Leadership

A major step in minimizing conflicts is achieved by keeping both staff and lay leaders involved in the daily or weekly interchange between host and guest ministries. Simply put, these leaders need to get to know one another. When there is both a spiritual and working relationship binding the two together, great strides in dissipating distrust are taken.

I'm an Anglo-American from Long Island, New York, and I knew little about the Brazilian people when I first arrived at NPBC. But as the senior pastor of a congregation that is host to more than 750 Brazilians, I had to make it my business to get to know them so as to dissipate any mistrust that comes with new leadership, especially when the new leader is from a foreign culture.

My interchange began with the Brazilian pastor and then branched out into his membership. After establishing a good relationship with him, I purposed to make inroads into his congregation. Soon afterward I had lunch with a guest family, then talked with their children about their transition into the American schools. This went a long way in breaking down barriers. My quest brought me to this realization: These are good people with strong Christian and family values that will truly complement our American church. This is an example of hands-on leadership that really minimizes conflicts, because the two parties know in their hearts that there is a genuine concern that binds them together. I believe the Lord would want me to expect nothing less from my staff members.

The Role of the Senior Pastor

The role of the host pastor should not include being a fireman constantly putting out small fires that flare up between the members of the host/guest or guest/guest groups. As a shepherd, a pastor's primary calling is to watch over and care for the sheep in his own flock. The duty of the host pastor is not to be embroiled in ironing out problems, or troubleshooting, between the host and guest or between the guests' fellowships (if you host more than one), since this will only diminish his effectiveness. His purpose, however, is to concentrate on his own ministry, which God called him to administrate.

Here are some suggestions on how the senior pastor can stay focused on his primary ministry:

1. Meet regularly with your guest pastors. Designate specific days and times of each week (e.g., Tuesday lunch with guest pastor #1; Saturday breakfast with guest pastor #2; or combine events) to discuss and straighten out any problems between fellowships that could not be resolved internally between themselves during the course of the week. The senior pastor should carefully consider how to resolve any problems that could not be settled internally.
2. Encourage your guest pastors to commission leaders to oversee their congregations and to be vigilant to spot any potential disagreements between guest groups that may give rise to a conflict.
3. Encourage your guest leadership to be autonomous. Remind them of their own empowerment to adjudicate any internal disputes.

Minimizing Conflicts

Setting boundaries to minimize conflicts will be treated by approaching the subject from two perspectives: first, minimizing the people conflicts, followed by minimizing the property conflicts.

Minimizing People Conflicts

The Sanctuary

The sanctuary is designed to be the place of worship and adoration of the Lord, but when sharing your church, it frequently becomes a staging area for the members to engage in hostilities. Violations of Christian courtesies can quickly agitate the latent nature of the *natural* man, causing him to react unspiritually. When the host or guest membership lazily files out of the sanctuary at the conclusion of their worship service at a mere crawl or without demonstrating good manners by not recognizing the other church brethren, feelings are easily hurt. Or if the host or guest churches foot traffic on the passageways between the sanctuary and the Sunday school classes becomes like a New York subway at rush hour where clogs prevent the proper transfer of people—like an obstacle course—members and visitors will not be endeared to your church.

The Kitchen

The breaking of bread is supposed to be one of the greatest blessings afforded the Christian, dating back to the first-century church (Acts 2:42). But in the shared church of today, the place where the eating takes place—the kitchen and the fellowship hall—the breaking of bread can become a conflict area. When two groups share the kitchen and have their own designated cabinets, the mere borrowing of a coffeepot could be viewed as an infringement of property rights. Leftover foods and paper products, together with unemptied trash cans, will undoubtedly raise the irritability between the host and guest groups.

The Parking Lot

Reportedly, the true test of spirituality comes when we leave the sanctuary and exit the church parking lot. Indeed, the parking lot can easily be transformed into a war zone when people are delayed (especially when the sermon went long and they're hungry) by discourteous or self-centered drivers. Add foul or hot weather to the scene, and the parking lot can easily become a flashpoint for motorized warfare. Overcrowding or the necessity to walk a long distance to the church can easily annoy members and discourage newcomers.

The Rest Rooms

One of the places that is often neglected and can discourage visitors from returning is the church's rest rooms. Untidy or unattended rest rooms are often viewed as representative slices of the entire ministry, often becoming the point of conversations on the way home.

Custodians cannot maintain constant surveillance of the rest rooms. This is why the leadership of both the host and guest church must participate in keeping the rest rooms presentable, especially during peak hours.

The Children

Unruly children or crying babies will disrupt the worship service or Bible study class. Their parents should not sit idly and observe but react to avoid unwittingly undermining the sermon or teaching.

Damage Control

The battle ground of the church is usually in the sanctuary, the place of worship. Because of this, satanic forces use every source of subterfuge to wear down the resolve of their enemy by attacking the strongest weapon in the arsenal of the Christian—the joy of the Lord (Neh. 8:10). Doctrinal disputes are too blatant for the enemy to attack, so a subtle assault is more effective: Harass the Christians with irritants so they criticize and blame one another; cause them to concentrate on their cultural differences. This will rob them of the joy of joint fellowship and weaken their ministry. Unwittingly, we fall prey to the enemy.

The apostle Paul suggests a way to bring conflict to an end: "Be devoted to one another in brotherly love. Honor one another above yourselves" (Rom. 12:10). Using this edifying passage as a framework, NPBC drafted its version of Paul's advice and incorporated it in the Christian Courtesy segment of our Covenant:

> Christian courtesy must prevail at all times. From the leadership on down to the congregation, respect for each other's

Unity becomes precious when you walk through conflict in order to reach it.
—Lynn Buzzard, *Leadership*, vol. 4, no. 3

worship service to Sunday school and fellowship gatherings must be upheld so that we vacate the building as expediently as possible to allow the other congregation's use, and while we are exiting, we must extend every courtesy to each other in the process. The passageways should be kept clear so as to allow proper transfer of people to other locations. Therefore, we welcome fellowshipping on the courtyard patios (not in the hallways or passageways).

This measure of damage control greatly reduced the conflict surrounding the scheduling of our sanctuary. Other options include the alternate A.M./P.M. use of the sanctuary to reduce the traffic.

Paul exhorted the church at Thessalonica to separate themselves from idlers who dishonor the Lord (2 Thess. 3:6–13). He further advised that those troublemakers who did not work should not get a handout—no freeloading. His emphasis seems to be on eating being related to work. No work, no food. Similarly, we believe at NPBC that those who eat in our kitchen should work at cleaning it up. This means that the American church cleans up after itself, as do the Brazilians. The clarification of this arrangement is elementary. We have assigned what is to be shared and what is designated solely for one ministry. At NPBC, separate cabinets have helped immeasurably with this issue. To avoid abuse or the presumption of abuse, certain kitchen items should not be shared (tablecloths, utensils, etc.). We are careful to respect one another's cabinets as a result. Other appliances such as the refrigerator, oven, microwave, coffee urns are shared once permission is granted from the owner.

In our parking lot we find numerous servants at their posts to ward off any militant drivers. Monitors with bright orange vests, along with cone markers to guide traffic, act to defuse parking lot tensions. Demarcation lines may be needed to distinguish between the host and guest churches. If your church has a serious traffic problem, you would do well to contact your local police department, and for a nominal fee, enlist their cooperation to direct traffic each time your church meets. This will also go a long way to ease neighborhood complaints.

It is impossible to predict and agree on all the possible conflict scenarios that can pop up before the covenants between host and guest are drawn up and signed. Problems such as the serving of wine instead of grape juice for communion, or dancing in the fellowship hall at a teen rally, for example, need to be settled on a case-by-case basis within the leadership.

As for unruly children, ushers should escort those that distract the congregation out of the sanctuary while the pastor is preaching. Parents should accompany middle school children during the worship service. Supervision of children is imperative and parent accountability will ensure success. A good word from Proverbs 29:15 that helps us here is "The rod of correction imparts wisdom, but a child left to itself disgraces his mother" (or ministry). Whatever strategy is used, the primary objective is always to protect the Word of God being preached from the pulpit so that it reaches the ears of the unregenerate visitor and edifies the believer. Everything else is incidental.

Minimizing Property Conflicts

The Sanctuary

After a worship service, the sanctuary should not look like a stadium after a rousing ball game. Posters, bulletins, unused offering envelopes, snack wrappers that are left behind from either the host or guest church give the appearance that the sanctuary is not revered as it should be. Constant rearranging of musical and sound equipment on the altar area should be minimized to avoid conflict.

The Fellowship Hall

Next to the kitchen is the fellowship hall, where the host and guest membership assemble to praise the Lord and talk about what God is doing in the church. When the guest ministry decorating committee decorates it to resemble a roller rink for the youth ministry rally and the rally runs overtime into Sunday morning, what becomes of the host church evangelism class scheduled to meet at 9:00 A.M.? Suppose the fellowship hall air-conditioning unit suddenly breaks down on Saturday night (after the guest group held a wedding reception) and the host church needs it for its Sunday luncheon. Who takes responsibility and who does damage control?

Unauthorized Expansions

Off-limit rooms that have been agreed upon by the leadership are frequent targets for ministry splinter groups seeking a secret hideaway for their equipment. Any vacant room or closet fit for storage is quickly spied out and filled with party decorations, stage paraphernalia, or left-over Christmas gear. Mysteriously, the culprits disappear without a trace. Border violations of this sort are common in joint ministries. When the guest group expands and surreptitiously pushes beyond their borders to occupy additional space, a leadership meeting needs to be called to settle the problem.

At NPBC, we have at our facility certain rooms that are considered "hallowed ground." One such room is the workroom of our retired custodian. This utility space is dedicated to his faithful memory and service. We use it to stash away all his old tools along with spare parts necessary for the repair of the buildings. One day the guest pastor asked me if they could convert it into a storage area to stockpile chairs. He might just as well have asked me if he could build a mosque on Solomon's temple! I immediately, yet graciously, refused.

Facility Use by Outside Groups

Allowing outside groups to use your facility for special events can bring serious legal ramifications if injuries occur. "Churches may be legally responsible for injuries occurring on their premises while being used by outside groups if they maintain sufficient 'control' over their premises during such use."[1] The senior pastor must be aware of the potential danger that can affect him if he is not mindful of this serious hazard.

Minor Annoyances

The indiscriminate duplication and distribution of keys rank high in this department. Violations in security wreak havoc in a ministry when keys are given to members and are then duplicated. So when articles or equipment are not where they are supposed to be, a duplicate key is often the culprit.

Unsupervised children or teens who noisily fill corridors on the way to the rest rooms only to loiter there will disrupt the peace and quiet of worship or Bible study. They, therefore, need to be kept under control for the sake of peace.

The deacons' closet can easily become the final resting place for posters, newsletters, bulletins, special offering envelopes, new member registration cards designed for dissemination among the congregation. This should also be kept under control, and the closet should remain free from clutter.

Damage Control

The pastor of our guest church and I disagreed over a property issue. After paying one thousand dollars and waiting four weeks for the arrival of our two new worship banners (the flamboyant type that hang on the wall in the sanctuary, with all the frills and trappings), we were naturally excited to assemble them and set them in a place of prominence in our sanctuary before the worship service. Coincidentally, the Brazilian church was holding a wedding on the day we purposed to install the banners. After we spent two hours installing the banners on the wall, the Brazilian church

The Fort Worth *Star-Telegram* reported that firefighters in Genoa, Texas, were accused of deliberately setting more than forty destructive fires. When caught, they stated, "We had nothing to do. We just wanted to get the red lights flashing and the bells clanging."

The job of firefighters is to put out fires, not start them. The job of Christians is to help resolve conflict (Matt. 5:9), not start more of it.

—Gerald Cornelius, *Leadership*, vol. 17, no. 1

objected on the grounds that they would interfere with their wedding decorations. Both sides saw red. A meeting was immediately convened to bring about a resolution of the conflict. Drawing on the God-centered relationship established over the past three years, the pastors were able to discuss the matter and extinguish the fire without so much as a whiff of smoke drifting near the membership. Once again, the God-honoring relationship in the leadership must prevail in order to make the sharing of your church successful.

Proper congregational training from the pulpit regarding the desecration of the sanctuary by litter or snack foods and drinks will reduce tensions between the host and guest churches. Bulletin inserts along with posters on the outside of sanctuary doors ("No Food or Drink") will promote keeping the sanctuary clean.

Scheduling of the fellowship hall for various events such as weddings, anniversaries, birthdays, harvest festivals (the Christian alternative to halloween), and the like should go through the host church administration office, which maintains an annual calendar that is designed to avoid planning conflicts and overlaps. A written reservation and approval form should be required to be signed by both the host and guest leadership. The Operations Covenant outlines the need for clean-up task forces for both host and guest church that should incorporate guidelines on the setting up and breaking down of all staging and decorations employed in either the fellowship hall or classroom.

When an incident develops, whether it be the failure of the air conditioner or any appliance, the group using the facility at the time should take immediate action to rectify the problem. One night at NPBC, the main sewer line collapsed while the Brazilian ministry was having a celebration. Fortunately, they had the presence of mind and the resources to gather several men together to dig up and locate the pipe and clear the blockage until it could be professionally and permanently repaired. According to the Shared Expense agreement, both the host and guest church divided the expenditure. This kind of cooperation keeps a shared ministry vibrant and operational. Cooperative work programs in a shared ministry include scheduled workdays that do more than clean up the facility. They build relationships, enthusiasm, trust, and ownership.

Unauthorized expansions frequently occur out of familiarity. The ideal ongoing relationship between host and guest may indeed promote incursions into the boundaries set in the agreement. Familiarity may lead to liberality and the relaxing of border rules. The author of Hebrews reminds us that brotherly love should continue despite infractions: "Keep on loving each other as brothers" (Heb. 13:1). Reiteration of the boundaries should then be followed up with the attitude of getting beyond the violation for the overall sake of harmony in the ministry. The use of the word "keep" in Hebrews certainly embraces Jesus' instruction on forgiveness. When Peter asked him how many times he should forgive his brother if he sins against him, Christ answered, "I tell you, not seven times, but seventy-seven times" (Matt. 18:22). Certainly the brethren should aspire to this goal.

Permission for outside groups (noncongregational members) to use your facility should be granted with caution. Scout troops, preschools, aerobics classes, substance abuse classes, and childbirth classes may hold a church legally responsible for injuries occurring on its premises. Lawsuits have been filed against churches when they held "sufficient control" over the event, and juries have handed down significant monetary awards against negligent churches. This is why at NPBC we have developed a *Church Property Liability Waiver*. This document provides limited protection to the ministry at NPBC (limited in the sense that any document can be challenged in a court of law) and is required for any event.

Christ's church is not exempt from border violations. In fact the Lord allows them to test our faith and our resolve to get along together in spite of the trespass. But we must endeavor to honor God through conflict. John Calvin summarizes the thought: "We ought not to dwell upon the vices of men, but rather contemplate in them the image of God, which by his excellence and dignity can and should move us to love them and forget all their vices which might turn us therefrom."

10

Dealing
with the Church Sign

One sunny morning, two months into my pastorate at NPBC, I decided to take a walk on the outside perimeter of the church property. Everything seemed in order until I came to where the church sign should be. I gasped as I realized that during the night the painted wood sign had disintegrated from weathering, then collapsed of its own weight and lay face down on the ground. I picked the panel off the ground and just chuckled to myself, "This must be a *sign* from the Lord that he wants us to put up a new sign!"

The next week I met with the pastor of the Brazilian church, our major tenant, and we agreed to shop for a commercial sign company that could build and erect a more suitable sign. That meeting was the beginning of a two-year saga over our sign!

The first problem we encountered was the message. "Sign language" was really key here! What did we want the sign to say? We agreed that the message should be one that communicated both our individuality and unity at the same time. So we decided on:

> † North Pompano Baptist Church
> † First Brazilian Baptist Church
> Ralph D. Curtin, Pastor   Silair Almeida, Pastor
> [Hours of Operation]

The message determined the size of the sign and, together with the style, determined the price. We agreed on the price tag of $5,200, which included fabrication, installation, the permit, and the electrical work. As per our agreement, we would split the cost of capital improvements that benefitted both ministries. Then we waited the two-month period for the sign permit to be approved and the construction to begin.

Finally, the happy day came when the sign was installed. Everyone rejoiced! However, the rejoicing was short-lived. Several weeks after the sign began proclaiming who we were, reports from our neighbors began to come in. The message on the sign was too confusing. Our neighbors, those people who live in the nearby community and drive or walk past the church two to five times a day, did not understand who we were. And since we care about what our neighbors (potential members) think about our church, we became concerned. They were asking: Are we an American church or a Brazilian church? Or are we a combination of both? Perhaps we are an American church with a Brazilian outreach or mission? We knew that nearly all of the Brazilians lived a considerable distance from the church, and since we were looking to build up our American church, the confusing message had to be corrected to attract those who wanted to visit the American church.

Importance of the Sign

James Berkley notes correctly, "The nonmember or visitor may view our facility as the most tangible expression of our faith. Thus, we will benefit from periodically looking at our church facilities through the eyes of a potential member. Does the structure look inviting? *Does our sign truly identify the church?*[1] (italics mine). That was our problem; the sign did not properly identify the church, and more correctly, *our* church. We were perplexed over what to do, so we left it alone for several months. But the sign problem continued to trouble me.

Sign Survey

Berkley's notes helped me considerably. He advises:

Church signs communicate an image that affects how members and potential attenders perceive the congregation. Untidy signs say "We don't care." Worse yet, if bulbs have failed, the paint has faded, or the surface has become overgrown by shrubbery, the sign may not be readable . . . does it communicate an image suited to the congregation? New insights can also be gained by having several people who do not attend church relate what the sign says to them.[2]

So with clipboard in hand, I set out to take a silent survey of a number of churches in the adjoining communities. Those churches that were sharing their buildings, what did their sign communicate? When I completed the survey, I approached our Brazilian pastor with my findings.

I explained that I found that many of the larger churches that shared their church had no mention of their guests on their sign. If they did, the guest church's designation occupied a very small percentage of the sign, or they had their own sign in a separate location so as not to detract from the statement on the host church's sign. My concerns heightened. In the back of my mind it occurred to me that I needed to bring in outside help to assist me with the dilemma. But based on my personal survey of neighboring churches, I thought it a good idea at present to modify the sign somewhat before conferring with outside sources. Accordingly, I went to the

Brazilian pastor with this concept: "Suppose we change the panel in the sign to read **'North Pompano Baptist Church'** in bold as the main text, then underneath our lettering put **'First Brazilian Baptist Church'** also in bold, only in Portuguese!" My thinking was that it would convey and clarify the message that we were both an American and Brazilian church. That is, Americans would simply not understand the Portuguese language—they would see only the English—while the Brazilian brethren would see the sign as their church as well. The Brazilian pastor scratched his head and reluctantly nodded in assent that it may help both churches. So we each paid $475 for another new panel with the new look.

Unfortunately for us, this move to revise the sign turned out to be a huge disappointment.

The NPBC Task Force

The turmoil over our sign most definitely developed into a quandary, but it wasn't our only dilemma. In the midst of our unfolding drama, our Haitian brethren, who also rent a small portion of our facility, became swept up in the sign frenzy and took it upon themselves to erect their own sign. One morning I arrived at the church to find a homemade sign fashioned out of a quarter sheet of plywood nailed to two two-by-fours, with each two-by-four standing in three concrete blocks. They proceeded to place the hand-painted placard on the side of the building they rent.

Once I explained to them that the county required a zoning permit, with approved drawings and surveys before any sign could be erected, they readily complied and dismantled the sign. But this incident along with several other developing situations provided me with the necessary impetus to finally put together a task force of outside sources.

The task force was multifaceted, inasmuch as I purposefully attempted to answer several nagging questions that seemed to be retarding the growth of the American ministry.

The perception of the sign was one of them. The candidates recruited for the task force came from numerous walks of life, and they all had been serving the Lord in other ministries. One was a retired pastor of a nearby church; two were Christian college professors (one woman, one man); a young married couple who were attending a Christian college while employed in a secular company also graced the list. In addition we also asked a young couple with children and a middle-aged couple who were dating and serving in another church to join in the task force. One of the questions in the questionnaire was pointedly directed at the sign: "What is your reaction to our sign on the lawn in the front of the building? What message does it give?"

The consensus confirmed my suspicion: The sign is too confusing. Now I had a deepening problem—what to do about it. I knew I had to correct the identity misinformation crisis, but deliberating with my church council over the task force findings didn't bring us to a resolution. Then it occurred to me: "Ask your pastor-friend Bob, who spent twenty years in commercial signs before becoming a pastor, about it." So I asked my friend Bob to join me for lunch one day and added casually, "Take a look at our sign on your way in and tell me what it says to you."

"Your sign is definitely telling everybody that this is a Brazilian church. Plain and simple," Pastor Bob announced as he walked in the door. I mulled over his response during lunch, but as far as I was concerned, that was the clincher for me. The following day I reviewed our financial statements, then announced a congregational meeting. At the meeting I explained the situation about the sign to our people and suggested that we reclaim full ownership of it by returning to the Brazilian church the money they invested. This would forever end the problem over the sign—it would be 100 percent ours. In addition, we would have to spend another nine hundred dollars to revise the sign panel to read only **"North Pompano Baptist Church."**

Once again the membership put their trust in me as their pastor and unanimously voted to return to the Brazilian church their financial investment in the sign. Then I had to break the news to the Brazilian pastor.

After I explained the developments and the results of the task force regarding the sign, I added in defense of my position that his church already had a membership of over 750 people and the number was steadily increasing. So building his membership was not really an issue that would be contingent on our sign. Then I reminded him that the Brazilian community did not reside in the church neighborhood, but in fact, several miles away. So advertising was not an issue, especially since they had their own church newspaper, in Portuguese, that had a very large circulation in the extended Brazilian district. He agreed with my reasons and accepted the refund.

Our experience has proved that signs should not be shared except under very careful scrutiny. Signs are extremely important and give a glaring message, and you want to be sure that the message of your church is clearly understood by your community.

Advice Concerning Your Sign

John Throop makes four key considerations when assessing an old sign or when planning a new one:[3]

1. **Purpose:** What do we want the sign to do?
2. **Setting:** What is the speed limit where the sign will be posted?
3. **Content:** Do we want a sign that only identifies the church name or one that can display specialized messages?
4. **Regulations:** What are the zoning regulations regarding signs?

All of these factors weigh heavily on the success of your sign. If your church is going to spend between three and six thousand dollars on a sign, you should maximize its effectiveness to get your money's worth!

Our *purpose* in erecting the sign was to make a statement to the neighborhood that our church was alive and well, standing firm while proclaiming the gospel of Jesus Christ. Our church went through a transition period for several years, during which the message and its mission became clouded. In addition, the appearance of the facility had been neglected, so we wanted the sign to remind the community that a great resurgence was taking place in our ministry.

The *setting* in our case was very good. Our church is located on a through street between two major arteries, in the middle of a major subdivision. This affords us maximum exposure; probably about fifty to sixty cars per hour pass our sign, and with a speed limit of thirty miles per hour, everyone is able to read it.

Our *content* is inviting! In addition to the sign logo identifying our church along with the pastor's name, it also displays a Bible message. The message on our sign is designed to catch the eye of motorists and pedestrians and remind them of spiritual themes. A typical message would be similar to: "No God, no peace. Know God, know peace." We change the message every two weeks.

Regulations can affect sign design. Your sign must conform to local zoning regulations. Signs that illuminate with changeable letters offer the greatest degree of exposure and the most versatility.

11

Maintaining Your Identity as the Host Church

The marks that America is going through an identity crisis are all around us. With the continuous influx of foreign nationals, America's traditional identity as a Judeo-Christian nation is quickly changing. In the corporate world, before the onslaught of imports, one could quickly recognize the identity of a company insignia or logo and know that the product was made in the USA. In the marketplace of today, shoppers really have to dig to identify items manufactured in America. In the individual life, too, finding our identity has become a major issue, with many people going to psychiatrists, psychologists, and Christian counselors. People are asking three basic questions: Who am I? Where am I going? How can I get there?

The Christian church is not immune from this modern-day phenomenon. Studies into belief patterns reveal that an identity crisis in the American Christian church has escalated tremendously. This accounts for the vast number of people who lack knowledge of the Bible and the hosts of Christians that reject the accuracy of Scripture and extol the virtues of good works while slamming both Christ's sinless nature and his solitary propitiation for sin. It seems they just don't know who they are or where they're going. The question of how they can get there doesn't suggest itself to them any longer.

If these questions are not properly answered, then the church will lose its focus, its direction, and its purpose. The church must know who it is, where it's going, and how to get there. When a church is the host for a guest group, its need to know its identity is that much greater. The host church's identity *must* be clear and maintained, or the church will fail.

Who Are You?

We at NPBC were fortunate to determine who we are early in my ministry. Since our church was already sharing its facility with the Brazilian group prior to my arrival, it was imperative for us to distinguish and maintain our identity without blending or straining each other's heritage. From the perspective of the possibility of assimilation, I did indeed determine at the outset of my ministry that their group was in no way a threat to the integrity of our church. There were no designs to merge the two groups. However, maintaining your identity when you share your church is an ongoing process.

The Vision for the Church Is Foundational

Maintaining the identity of your church must begin with the Holy Spirit. The leadership must have a complete vision of what God's purpose is for your church. God's message to his people is clear: "Where there is no vision, the people perish" (Prov. 29:18 KJV). As a pastor or leader you must grasp God's vision for your ministry and allow his Spirit to direct you. Insisting on a vision for the church will bring clarity to your identity. George Barna, in *The Power of Vision*, writes, "The absolute goal of vision for ministry is to glorify God. It is not numerical growth."[1] This statement along with

Proverbs 29:18 should help you formulate a vision statement. It may read something like this: "Our desire is to have God's people follow the example described in Scripture of a commitment to reach the lost and to train other believers to imitate Christ, His Word, life and deed through worship, evangelism, discipleship, ministry and fellowship."[2]

The vision statement should be foundational. Then you must build your mission statement on it. This statement gives your church its purpose to exist. A model mission statement may look like this: "To advance the growth and development of Christ's disciples through instruction in the Word of God so that we may effectively reach the souls of men with the Bible's message of salvation (Ps. 138:2; Matt. 4:19; 28:19–20)."[3] Once your church has the *vision* and *mission* statements in place, you can then answer the question of who you are.

Decide Who You Want to Be

What kind of a church do you want to be? Do you want to be a culturally mixed congregation where various ethnic backgrounds and languages are brought together in one ministry in one church? Or do you want to celebrate cultural diversity while maintaining individual identity—separating the groups under one church? These questions branch out into others: What image do you want to project into your surrounding neighborhood? What do you want the unchurched to think about your church? Do you want your church to be known as an American church? An American-Brazilian church? An American-Brazilian-Haitian church? Naturally, the people you will attract to your ministry will be determined by the kind of church you want to be. Whatever your choice is, you should find a biblical platform to support it.

Your church must maintain its separate identity and individuality apart from the group who is sharing your church. Merging the two culturally different churches is a concept that I believe does not have a biblical basis. We do, however, find tribal distinctions in the Old Testament that provide us with a restrictive model to follow. Unless you are certain that God did indeed call you to be a copastor with a foreign church by joining your two congregations into one at the expense of blending and straining your heritage, I strongly urge you not to do it. However, if your spirit testifies that God did call you to be the singular leader of your American-based group, then you have the confidence of God. This will safeguard the future of the church God has called you to.

The Model of Early Israel

If we are American-born, we can call ourselves American. Or if we are from a foreign country but presently live in one of the fifty United States, we too can call ourselves American. The early Israelite economy, in which God ordained the separation of tribes, is a prototype of our own. From this example we learn that it is important to uphold unity while remaining distinctly separate.

When we look at the theology behind the Old Testament tribal system, the twelve tribes of Jacob were all of the nation of Israel, all believing in and worshiping the same God, yet remaining individual tribes. Beginning with Moses, the tribal structure continued into the New Testament period. *Nelson's Bible Dictionary* defines the tribe as

> a social group composed of many clans and families, together with their dependents, outside the ties of blood kinship, who had become associated with the group through covenant, marriage, adoption or slavery. The nation of ancient Israel, especially at the time of the events recorded in the Book of Judges, was a tribal society (Num. 1; 2; 26; Josh. 13:1–21:45; Judg. 19:1–21:25).[4]

The expanded definition includes:

> The tribal confederation with its institutions reached its highest form during the period recorded in the books of Joshua and Judges. The rigidity of Israel's tribal structure did weaken somewhat with the establishment of the United Kingdom

under David and Solomon. But tribal organization and association was maintained throughout later biblical history (Luke 2:36; Acts 4:36; Rom. 11:1; Heb. 7:14).

The elders in each tribe maintained the internal administration and guidance of the people throughout the period leading up to and after the exile, while in the New Testament mention is made as to tribal ancestry, indicating the strong, ongoing emphasis on tribal custom.

Two Separate Entities, Yet One

Further evidence of the concept of maintaining individuality while being united is found in Paul's teachings. Paul explains that both the Jew and the Gentile are now one in Christ, for Christ has broken down the middle wall (rendered *fence* or *barrier*) that separated the two in the Old Testament economy (Gal. 3:26–28; Eph. 2:11–14). We are now able to worship God in Christ together. Although we are now counted as one, we do, in fact, remain individual, separate entities.

We know this is true because Paul is building on the view God presented in the Old Testament of both man and woman and the nation of Israel seen as compound unities. In Genesis 2:24 God says, "For this reason a man will leave his father and mother and be united to his wife, and they will become one flesh." We have two separate entities, a man and a woman, yet God sees them as *one*. The Hebrew word for *one* used here is *echad,* which is a compound unity in contrast to the Hebrew word *yachid,* which also means *one,* but a solitary *one* (rendered "only one," Zech. 12:10). Therefore in God's eyes, a man remains a man, a woman remains a woman, each with their own separate body, soul, and spirit, but when they marry, they are reckoned as one unit.

This is further demonstrated in Ezekiel 37:15–17, where the prophet explains that in the mind of God he sees the two tribes of Judah and Ephraim as *one*. The same Hebrew word for *one (echad)* is used here, denoting that although the tribes are independent of one another, they are spiritually joined by

God's Spirit just as husband and wife are through the act of matrimony.

These examples represent models that God used to show how his church should be established: Maintain your own separate identity like a limb or organ, yet come together as one body in Christ.

Ownership and Control

In addition to the possibility of having its identity endangered, the host church may in time face the dilemma of being displaced by the guest group, which may eventually lead to relinquishing ownership in its building. This may never apply or it may seem preposterous to the congregation just starting its inquiries into the possibilities of sharing its church, but in time it could become a reality.

Displacement through population growth is a real concern when it comes to sharing your church, even if there is no immediate or long-term threat to ownership. It is possible for the host church to abdicate its identity when the guest membership overpowers it. If the guest church gets to the point that it dwarfs the host church, the questions that arise are, Does sheer size constitute ownership? Who's in charge, the larger of the two groups or the group who holds the deed to the property? The surrendering of rooms and space to the guest group may, in its own inimical way, advance the school of thought that fosters the adage, "possession is nine-tenths of the law." Human nature views superior quantities of people as strength, dominance, and control, bringing feelings of subordination to those of fewer numbers.

The solution to this problem is somewhat sensitive. Sensitive in the sense that members of your guest group can easily be wounded when this subject is addressed. Their response would probably be to dispute any notion that displacement is taking place. Otherwise, they might unwittingly incriminate themselves and matters could worsen. Although their feelings can be hurt, the utmost consideration must be granted in favor of the host church. They must be afforded the highest level of protection.

When displacement threatens the host church while an Operations Covenant (see chapter 8) is in place, then a meeting between host and guest leadership is warranted to review and reiterate their joint policy, followed by working to dismantle any identity problem. Discussions should revolve around alternative expansion options that are designed to safeguard the host church from sacrificing its identity. Reminding the guest group of its responsibility to honor its pledge not to ask for additional space would be in order. At NPBC we solved the problem of displacement through a clause in our Operations Covenant entitled "Spatial Parameters." This written agreement settles any disputes that come up.

Outside Concerns

Churches are often petitioned by American community organizations to use their facilities for various functions. Groups such as the Boy Scouts, your local pregnancy awareness advocacy group, or a Christian college may ask for access to your building. If your available space is already allocated to the guest group, worthwhile outside organizations would be denied the opportunity of using your church site.

Relinquishing Ownership

Sharing your church does not mean that the guest group is going to take it over. Population displacement does not mean your church is being taken over. Merging your church with another group does not mean the guest group is going to take your church over either. Entering into a joint-ownership arrangement with a guest group does not mean the host church has surrendered. But the actual transferring of the deed to the guest church *does* represent the abdication of your church to another group. Your church may never be exposed to any of these possibilities, but nevertheless, they do exist and we should explore them.

Merging

Suppose you are a start-up church that has been meeting in a local elementary school on Sundays for almost three years. Your denominational state association has been subsidizing you as a mission church, but that support will end at the end of the year. The congregation is expanding below the nominal rate, but because the overhead is low, the expenses, along with the pastor's modest salary, are presently being met. You have your own church name registered with the county and are hopeful that your ministry will grow to the point when one day you can support yourself and consider purchasing your own building. But the impending loss of funds from the state association brings ominous feelings of fear and possible failure into your heart, so you ask God's Spirit for guidance. Then one day you receive a call from a pastor-friend whose ministry is thriving, and he casually lets you know that he needs an associate pastor to minister to his church family. He then makes an offer to have you merge with his church. He reminds you of the security you will enjoy while working together in his ministry. You weigh the offer, pray about it, then decide to present it to your struggling congregation. They admit to the potential hazards the church may face and decide that it would be best if the group did merge with the stronger church. Is there anything unusual with this scenario? No, there is not. This is a common occurrence in mission work and churches that are unable to sustain themselves.

Yet such a move can severely impact a church's identity. The identity and ownership of the start-up church will be absorbed in the larger or sending church. In reflection, the start-up church pastor will undoubtedly ask himself if he heard the Lord correctly when he began his mission church in the school, since it didn't work out. But is that the right question to ask? His initial endeavor was used of the Lord for a purpose that may never be revealed. Who can tell the long-range effect his ministering had on the sheep that were in his flock during that time he was their shepherd?

Joint Ownership

Making the decision to enter into a joint-ownership agreement with your guest church is one of the highest magnitude, requiring the full approval of the host congregation. Unless 100 percent of your membership agrees, it is not a good idea to proceed, since God may be saying "no," or "not now."

A fellow pastor from a nearby church telephoned me one day to ask my advice about the inner workings of sharing a church with a group from a foreign culture. His church had taken in a minority group months earlier, and he wanted to draw from my experiences in this area before his church proceeded with a formal, permanent arrangement. During the discussion that followed, I learned that his church council was on the verge of legally changing the ownership of their church buildings to include the guest group. Their buildings would be held in joint ownership as well as their checking account and all their financial holdings. Any future tithes and offerings would be pooled together. The leadership of each group would stay the same. He would remain the pastor over the American group, the other pastor over the guest group. When I asked what the guest group was bringing to the table, that is, what monetary or financial investment they would be making to solidify this arrangement, he said they'd bring just their future tithes and offerings. The purpose for embracing them, he went on to say, would be to help them out and give them a place to stay.

I was intrigued by this reasoning, so I inquired further. He told me that the guest group had been sharing their church in the past, but things got out of hand and they had to evict them. He informed me that the leadership became too possessive and that their children were totally unruly, setting a poor example to the children in the American church.

"And you took them back and now you're thinking about transferring half the ownership of the buildings—your entire church—to them?" I asked incredulously.

"Well," he answered, groping for words because he realized the folly of the idea. "They had no other place to go and combining sounded like a good idea at the time."

This is an example of making a decision for joint ownership with another group for the wrong reasons. A joint-ownership compact involves the combining of two groups using a bilateral transfer document that will include all property, assets, and ministry management. Normally this is done for the purpose of sharing a facility to reduce expenses. Maintaining separate ministries while operating under a joint-ownership agreement is another way of accomplishing this goal.

An elementary question that should be addressed to the committee contemplating a joint-ownership covenant is, What is the host church's responsibility to the founding fathers? Will the congregation feel that they betrayed their patriarchs when the church is legally joined with another? Many of your present members may indeed be part of the original congregation and could voice such an objection. For them, to surrender the church's identity is tantamount to heresy. On the other hand, they may consider the times in which we live, and be of the persuasion that the traditional church of their fathers must yield to the present-day contemporary church that is obliged to share its facility to advance the kingdom of God. For them, to join ownership would just be an extension of their mission statement.

Actual Transfer

The host church may experience seasons of unusual growth patterns, during which it appears that God is blessing the guest ministry more abundantly. The guest church may be undergoing tremendous numerical expansion while the host church remains relatively stable; perhaps they're even struggling to exist. This may be construed as a sign from God that the guest church entertain and explore the possibility of taking over the entire facility as their own. This would mean that the guest church actually buys the entire facility

> Remember, it's Christ's church, not ours. Jesus founded the church, died for the church, sent his Spirit to the church, and will someday return for his church. As the owner of the church, he has already established the purposes, and they're not negotiable.
>
> —Rick Warren, *The Purpose-Driven Church*[5]

from the host church. The host church would then transfer its ownership and relocate its ministry to other quarters.

At first the host church may be repulsed at the notion of selling its building. The mere suggestion may cause the core group to cringe and cry, "Never!" However, to find out what the mind of the Lord is, the same fundamental questions mentioned in the above categories should be asked. But now, in view of the enormity of the issue, a feasibility study must also be conducted.

Feasibility Study

A feasibility study is a comprehensive analysis that considers all aspects of selling your present church facility and relocating somewhere else. This requires the nomination of committed members to form a task force to determine whether or not it would behoove the host church to make such a move. The task force should perform the following functions prior to presenting the suggestion to sell the church to the congregation for approval:[6]

1. Assign a prayer warrior group to seek direction from the Lord.
2. Acquire at least two bona fide real estate appraisals of the host church's present building(s) and property.
3. Determine the target area for relocation.
4. Ascertain if the distance to the target area is traversable for the existing congregation.
5. Perform an in-depth study of the target area that must include both an economic and demographic profile to assess future growth potential.

6. Discover if an existing building is available in the target area to suit the purpose of your church, or whether it is practical to build a new facility.
7. If a new building is chosen, a temporary residence will be required until the new facility is built.
8. Inquire from a general contractor the cost estimate for your new building. The price of securing new land would be added to this amount.
9. Project your attrition rate. How many members do you expect to lose in the transition?
10. Require the task force to *agree on all points* before presenting the proposal to the congregation.

Building Ownership

If discussions about the actual transfer of the building have progressed to where a feasibility study should be undertaken, then the question as to who really owns the building must be addressed to suppress discontent and bitterness from brewing within the congregation.

In the New Testament, Paul affirms the truth that God's building is made up of his body of believers (1 Cor. 3:9, 16–17; 2 Cor. 6:16; 1 Tim. 3:15), making it clear that the building is nothing more than a meeting place without the body of Christ to fill it with the Holy Spirit. Therefore, the body of believers, on the one hand, belongs to God. On the other hand, since the building was constructed and maintained by the funds from God's people, the building does belong to God as well. He, the omnipotent God, can do whatever he wills with his property, despite how foolish the action may appear to mere mortals.

The host church must recognize that when the staff leadership together with the feasibility study task force unanimously agree, and their findings conclusively point in the direction of actual transfer, this confirmation must be from God. An explanation for this principle can be found in the Book of 1 John: "Dear friends, if our hearts do not condemn us, we have confidence before God" (1 John 3:21). With this confidence, the host congregation should go forward in selling the church building to the guest congregation.

12

Where Are You Going and How Do You Get There?

As you have seen, recognizing *who you are* is the first step in maintaining your identity as the host church. Once this is established, the next question is *where are you going?* You will recall that finding out *who you are* required that you identify both your vision and your mission statement. To find out where you are going, we must now consider purpose.

Discover the Blessing

Recognizing how and where God is blessing your church will help you to discover your purpose. To do this, the host church must reflect on and contrast the relationship it once had with the relationship it is now enjoying with the guest church.

At NPBC, the guest Brazilian church emerged from a home Bible study and within a brief period grew to approximately seventy-five people. Soon afterward, they took up residence at our church. Our sanctuary seats over 750, so to concentrate the group in order to promote the sense of community during their worship service, the leadership cordoned off our three rows of pews and herded the group into one row of pews. Certainly, a small beginning. The Brazilian pastor hoped that one day the sanctuary would be filled with his people, and God, in fact, did honor his desire. Today, some six years later, the church is filled beyond capacity.

Great faith brings great rewards (Gen. 15:1). This truth has been borne out in the Brazilian church in many ways: (1) they are now the largest Brazilian church in North America, (2) they presently are building a two-million-dollar multipurpose building (on an adjacent piece of our property they purchased from NPBC), (3) they are one of the first Brazilian churches in America to adapt their entire ministry methods to the Purpose-Driven Church, which is the method that is the driving force behind the ministry at Saddleback Valley Community Church, founded by Rick Warren, (4) their annual monetary contributions to missions in Florida rank among the highest, (5) they are the central quarters for the Brazilian consulate in South Florida.

We at NPBC would be foolish not to recognize God's blessing on them. Their ministry and, no doubt, the ministries of many other culturally different groups are an example to the American people on how to build a church. Their zeal for the Lord, along with their boundless love for the Word of God, is truly inspiring. Numerous evangelism programs that involve both adults and youth act as a vehicle to transport the unchurched Brazilian community into their ministry where trained, vigilant counselors lead them to Christ. From there, they are nurtured in their discipleship classes until they are ready to begin their service for God. In many ways they model the first-century church.

Now you should ask your church this question: Are we better off with the guest ministry or without them? If the relationship between host and guest church is from the Lord, the answer will be in the affirmative.

Discover Your Purpose

Recognizing that your guest church has blessed your ministry is a road mark pointing you in the proper direction toward discovering your purpose. Again, as Rick Warren points out, "We don't decide the purposes of the church—we *discover* them."[1] The next step is to compare your vision and mission statements with those of the guest church to arrive at a common denominator. At NPBC our common denominator can be reduced to four words: (the) Word, evangelism, discipleship, service. These four words provide the framework for our purpose statement:

1. The Word of God is our Measurement
2. Evangelism is our Mission
3. Discipleship is our Mentorship
4. Service is our Ministry

Combined, the statement reads: We *measure* all things by the Scriptures so we can fulfill our *mission* of reaching souls to *mentor* them for future *ministry*.

Our statement is the driving force behind our ministry thrust. It provides a compass for every program. Your purpose statement will reveal the direction your church should be moving in. We can state the terms in equation form:

VISION + MISSION = PURPOSE

Divergent Targets, United Purpose

Careful analysis of your evangelism methods will reveal your target audience, which should reaffirm your identity. At NPBC, I have observed and evaluated the method the Brazilian church uses to build its ministry and have concluded that its purpose is to draw its congregation from *outside* our community. Our guest ministries do not evangelize or minister to the immediate neighborhoods, but draw from their cultural community some fifteen to thirty miles away. By comparing their targets with the target audience we were attempting to focus on, we were able to arrive at our purpose.

At NPBC we discovered our purpose through various trial ventures. We placed newspaper ads in adjacent towns to attract the seeker or the unchurched from that town. We invested large sums of money on printing and postage for colorful brochures and catchy flyers to be sent to adjacent neighborhoods. We scanned the new mortgage lists for newcomers to the adjacent communities and sent them letters and flyers inviting them to our newly renovated church. All these methods failed because we came to realize that God wants us to minister to our *immediate* community. We discovered our purpose by comparison: *divergent targets* (host and guest churches reach different communities), yet *united purpose* (to reach the lost for Christ).

We discovered at NPBC that our direction in ministry is to reach the immediate community—the neighborhood that surrounds our church—for Christ. We discovered that our vision, mission, and purpose is to identify with the community in which God has placed us.

God's Holy Spirit often uses people's trials and errors to help them discover the direction he wants them to travel. In your church this identity evaluation process may take a different form, but the end result should bring you to the same destination point—reaching the lost for Christ. This enables us to complete our equation:

VISION + MISSION + PURPOSE = IDENTITY

How Do You Get There?

Of the three questions, Who are you? Where are you going?, and How do you get there?, Jesus made it easy for us to answer the last. In Matthew 4:19 he simply said, "Come, follow me, and I will make you fishers of men." Throughout

---

NPBC COMMUNITY SURVEY

We at North Pompano Baptist Church care about you! Would you please take a few minutes to complete this survey? Thank you!

1. What role do you think a neighborhood church can play in your life?
2. Why would you attend a church (or not attend a church)?
3. Are you currently a member of a local church?
4. What are your most pressing needs at this time?
5. Are you looking for a church that would fortify family values?
6. What is your impression of NPBC as a neighborhood church?
7. Do you think it is important for children to attend Sunday school?
8. Would you be interested in attending support groups that might meet at NPBC (e.g. Mothers of Preschoolers (MOPS); Bible Study, etc.)? Feel free to offer suggestions.
9. Why do you think many people don't attend church?
10. Can we include you in our regular mailing list?

Optional Personal Information:

Name: _____

Address: _____

Phone: _____ Best time to call: _____

---

the Gospels, Jesus repeats this command, "follow me," twenty times. Clearly, by following Jesus we will get to where we're supposed to go. This injunction, together with your purpose statement, dictates the method that enables you to be fishers of men. It is called your outreach program. Your entire church curriculum may revolve around outreach as opposed to any other program agendas, and if so, I have every confidence that the Lord will bless that work for his kingdom.

At NPBC our outreach program is designed to cultivate community awareness that we are an American church with a burning passion for the lost. We approach our outreach program from various angles: tract and flyer distribution, Jesus video presentations/surveys in the home, door-to-door surveys, and holiday events. While our distribution and survey program follows the "Go!" command of the Great Commission, the holiday events are intended to follow the Old Testament example of "Come and see" by providing a Christian alternative to a particular calendar holiday. This will act as a net to draw in the fish to your church.

Guest Church: Draw or Drain?

Your guest group is either a draw or a drain in helping you maintain your identity. If they represent a drain or a hindrance, you as the host church must help them overcome that problem. By working side by side with the guest ministry you can help them minimize their deficiencies. You must remember it is what Christ wants that's important: "Verily I say unto you, Inasmuch as ye have done it unto one of the least of these my brethren, ye have done it unto me" (Matt. 25:40 KJV).

13

When to Call In a Mediator

Several years ago, one of our guest groups showed disregard for the appearance and maintenance of the building they were renting on our church property. Discussions and letters failed to bring about a favorable resolution, so as senior pastor, I had no choice but to give them the ultimatum to either comply with our request to repair their building or to leave the church compound.

The crisis began to unfold when I made a visual inspection of both the interior and exterior of their separate building during our renovation program. This examination was warranted in keeping with the overall spirit of the restoration process that was taking place at the church facility at that time. Out of the three ministries that share our church grounds, each having their own rented building, this group saw no need to perform any repairs or restorative work but was quite content with the dilapidated condition both inside and out.

From the inspection, I made an exterior and interior repair list that had to be completed within ninety days.[1] Exterior areas included replacing the termite-infested wooden exit doors with metal ones, replacing the rotten fascia boards along with the roof vent screening, replacing the dead grass with live sod, painting the outside of the building. Interior items included clearing dangerous debris from fire exits, installing ceiling lights, removing an inoperable commercial stove from the kitchen, renovating the rest rooms so they are serviceable (repair plumbing and electric to code), resurfacing the office area floors with either tile or carpet, replacing crumbling Sheetrock.

After thirty days a follow-up inspection was made. This group then received a letter from me indicating that "our church council met and discussed the overall condition of your facility and many members expressed concern that the condition of the building has only slightly improved. As a church, we want to remind you that if there is no substantial improvement you will then be asked to vacate the premises in sixty days."

Another thirty days passed and no significant amount of work had been completed. After considering the significant cultural disparity as a possible cause of their laxity, I was persuaded that the group's mind-set bordered on rebellion against authority. They just did not want to be bothered to do the repair work. Nevertheless, our council met once again with their leadership to review the progress being made on the projects, reiterating our request and time constraints, and once again their apathetic posture was apparently unchanged.

It soon became apparent to me that God was up to something. He was going to use this crisis as a growth experience for both the host and guest church. The host church would learn to be firm while applying love and understanding of the different cultures, and the guest group would learn the need to be responsible for what God had allowed them to use. But that was still to come. For now, it was time to call on a mediator to intervene between the two parties for the purpose of reconciling them. As sinners, we have been reconciled to God through Christ our mediator (1 Tim. 2:5), and at times we do require some intervening process, act, or person to reconcile person to person.

Fortunately, in our denomination, we have intermediaries in the association of churches that stand ready to help in a time of need. One of their many purposes is to promote church unity between the American and ethnic groups in South Florida. With this in mind, I asked the director to personally handle this difficult situation. Within two weeks, a formal assembly was convened around the NPBC conference table, and the mediator who presided over the meeting, realizing the severity of the problem, brought a sense of urgency to the table. It was incumbent upon him to reinforce the host church's position, while applying a high level of diplomacy to gain the confidence of the guest group.

At the meeting, the presence of God's Spirit was apparent. The guest group began to realize the sweeping vision God had given me as the senior pastor to rebuild the church, and that their cooperation was greatly needed. The mediator served as the go-between to bring the two cultures together, and his sensitivity to the issues brought about a speedy resolution that has lasted to this day.

This kind of problem is not uncommon in Christ's church today. Despite the many biblical injunctions to uphold unity, complications can spring up that mandate bringing in an outside force to help in the negotiations and to realign the two groups.

Lessons in Reflection

Looking back at this crisis, I have observed several red flags along the way that could have helped us avoid this confrontation.

1. There was no arrangement to meet with this group's leadership for prayer, fellowship, and conferencing.
2. There was no Operations or Shared Expense Covenant in place.

3. There was little effort on the host church's part to understand the guest church's culture and how it was at variance with American culture.
4. Language difficulties along with misinterpreted directions raised barriers that seemingly took on the appearance of rebellion.
5. Consultation over any former agreements that were impractical and could not be honored was never done.
6. The lines of communication were not open.

When two families share the same house, there will be problems regardless of how much love and affection they have for each other. Likewise, there will be problems when two ministries share the same house of worship.

Satan's Diversionary Tactics

As we have seen, God's Spirit promotes and craves unity in the church. The enemy, however, promotes discord to tarnish the testimony of the church. Satan's tactics are often blatant and easily identifiable, but in our society today, he seems to be working undercover to undermine unity between the brethren. Samuel Chadwick's observation reminds us of Satan's course of action.

The Christian religion begins in a New Birth in the power of the Spirit. It is developed under His guidance, and sustained by His presence; but ignoring the Spirit, it becomes a matter of education and evolution. The Church is the Body of Christ begotten, unified, and indwelt by the Spirit, *but forgetting the Spirit, men wrangle over limbs, functions, and orders.* The Christian religion is hopeless without the Holy Spirit.[2] (italics mine)

When we forget to include the Holy Spirit in our daily operation of the church, we will slip into the carnal pit—doing Satan's work—by wrangling over *limbs, functions, and orders.* The precious time we could be spending to build up the body of Christ will be devoted to tearing it down. God's Spirit must sustain the work of the church and lead us away from majoring in the minors.

Iron Sharpens Iron

A principle that is alluded to in Scripture is that we can learn from our own mistakes or we can choose the wiser course and learn from the mistakes of others. In Scripture, the Holy Spirit carefully recorded the mistakes the patriarchs and the children of Israel committed, for the purpose of teaching us lessons so we could avoid the same costly errors.

This is why it is so important that when difficulties in sharing our church come along, we remember that there are other churches who have experienced similar troubles and, by the grace of God, handled them in a proper fashion without bringing serious injury to their ministry or to the church at large. Proverbs 27:17 reminds us, "As iron sharpens iron, so one man sharpens another." We can learn from each other's mistakes to minimize future ones.

Working through the Difficulty

Complainers and murmurers in Scripture failed to recognize God's purpose in difficult trials and hardships (Num. 11:1; 14:2–3) and were severely punished for their lack of faith in the Lord. That failure manifested itself in unfair comparisons, grumbling attitudes, and cutting remarks against God or his appointed leaders. "In all things God works for the good of those who love him, who have been called according to his purpose" (Rom. 8:28). God advises us not only to look beyond the difficulty but to work through it for the greater good of the church. Jim Cymbala counsels, "God does not always take us *out of difficulty;* many times he takes us *through it.*"[3] When God brings an event into the life of your church that threatens the church's very existence, he may not remove the difficulty (at least not right away), but watch carefully to see how his people deal with it. As we noted earlier in chapter 8, God is not interested in how we care for our buildings or programs but how we treat people. In the kingdom, God works through people to bring about his purposes. We must not lose sight of this important precept when difficulties arise, but we must take every precaution to protect the body of Christ.

When to Call In a Mediator

It is unrealistic to expect that different groups (especially with varied cultures) can share a church without experiencing some problems. While it is always best to settle our internal disputes quickly (Matt. 5:25) and without involving other parties, predicaments do occur that require outside help. Scenarios that indicate the need for an intermediary include:

1. When the guest church disregards the host church's spiritual authority. As long as the requests of the host church are in accordance with the Word of God, the guest church should comply (Exod. 14:10–15). Quarreling with the host church's authority is biblically wrong (Num. 20:3).
2. When the guest group continuously complains about the host church, despite the host church's efforts to accommodate them (Exod. 15:22–26; Num. 11:1–3; 14:27; 21:5).
3. When the guest church makes ongoing comparisons that are unfair, or when the guest ministry complains about God's provision for them regarding their quarters in your church, either comparing their former agreements with another church or expecting the host church to honor arrangements made by other ministries (Exod. 16:2–3; 17:1–7).
4. When the guest group incessantly groans against God (Ps. 77:1–9).

5. When the guest group refuses to join in the Operations Agreement or to establish a Shared Expense Agreement, or when they fail to comply with these agreements.
6. When there is a total breakdown of communication.
7. When there is an unresolved event that transpires in the guest congregation that will cast aspersions or shame on the host congregation (2 Cor. 6:3).

What the Mediator Should Accomplish

The intermediary should accomplish the goal of over-powering negative negotiations and power struggles by the introduction of new ideas with a fresh view toward unity. Chip Zimmer writes:

> Mediators don't judge conflicts. They simply try to facilitate negotiation, helping people examine issues from a Christian perspective and work toward a resolution pleasing to God. Mediators must remain neutral and can't be advocates for one side or the other. On biblical matters, however, Christian mediators must be advocates for the truth. They can't be neutral regarding the basic principles of Christian living.[4]

The mediator should also avoid rehashing the same rhetoric, conflicts, and discussions, and instead should act in an advisory capacity while moving the agenda at a steady pace into the settlement stage. When the magnitude of the problem necessitates a mediator, simply restoring the relationship will be grossly inadequate. Resolutions should be put in place to safeguard against future violations and breakdowns.

Safeguards

God has established a system of safeguards to follow in order to keep confrontations from reaching the level that requires a mediator.

1. A problem-solving council should be instituted as soon as the guest group is embraced. Joint delegations from both the host and guest church should agree to meet periodically to discuss any ongoing problems. This truth is reinforced in Scripture, "Where there is no counsel, the people fall, but in the multitude of counselors, there is safety" (Prov. 11:14 NKJV; also see 15:22).
2. Written covenants must be installed to protect the host-guest relationship (Deut. 31:24–26).
3. The guest group must be invited to take possession of their allotted space of the facility. Ownership goes beyond a mere financial investment; it must include a state of mind that "your house is our house." This will promote the appropriate treatment of church property (Num. 33:53–54).
4. Regularly scheduled meetings between the leadership of host and guest churches should be held whether or not they are needed. Once per month should be the minimum interval. This commitment will safeguard against a build-up of offenses or stumbling blocks toward one another (2 Cor. 6:3–4).
5. The host church must be responsible for maintaining proper communication with the guest group. The key to avoiding major problems is minimizing each point of conflict through rapid communication. A quick response to a problem will circumvent escalation (Matt. 5:25).

Reconciliation is one of the important themes Christ teaches in his Sermon on the Mount (Matt. 5:23–26), bringing out the command to first make things right between you and your brother (for our purposes, between host and guest) before bringing your gift of worship before God. In other words, reconciliation takes priority over worship. If indeed we are obedient, we should never reach the place where we require a mediator. Jay Adams observes:

> Problems between Christians should not continue unresolved. When they do, strength is sapped from the congregation and

members work at cross-purposes. Unresolved problems hurt everyone and dishonor Christ's name. There is no place, therefore, for such loose ends in the church. God does not allow for loose ends; rather He insists that every personal difficulty that arises must be settled. Whatever comes between Christians must be removed. Every such difference must be cleared up by reconciliation. And, for that purpose, God graciously provided a method by which this can be accomplished.[5]

That method by which we can achieve reconciliation applies both individually to the Christian and corporately to the church. That method is spelled out in Matthew 18 where Christ instructs on church discipline:

> "If your brother sins against you, go and show him his fault, just between the two of you. If he listens to you, you have won your brother over. But if he will not listen, take one or two others along, so that 'every matter may be established by the testimony of two or three witnesses.' If he refuses to listen to them, tell it to the church."
>
> verses 15–17

Pointedly, Christ advises that (1) the host church leader must approach the guest church leader privately when a problem arises and make every effort to settle the issue (this may require more than one try—even to the point of exhaustion). If that meeting(s) is unsuccessful and the guest leader remains adamant or unmovable, Jesus further urges that (2) the host pastor/leader must take one or two others from his staff to seek reconciliation once again. If this last-ditch effort fails, (3) the host pastor must bring in a mediator to address the problem in a larger forum.

14

Asking Your Guests to Leave

God's best, as prescribed in Scripture, is for the brethren to dwell in unity. The apostle Paul urges Christ's church to exercise cooperation and to draw together: "May the God who gives endurance and encouragement give you a spirit of unity among yourselves as you follow Christ Jesus" (Rom. 15:5). Unfortunately, that is not always possible. Despite Paul's exhortation, a spirit of unity does not always prevail, and sharing your church does not always work. When the spirit of unity is extinguished between the host and guest, it may be necessary to ask your guests to leave.

Now someone might say, "The Christian thing to do is to keep trying and make it work—continue to share with them what God has given you!" But the answer to this problem is not that simple.

A relevant story I read while doing research for this book describes the level of frustration a host church can reach that often precedes the decision to ask the guest church to leave.

"We'll never do that again!" The battle-scarred pastor looked me straight in the eye. "Nothing is worth that mess." For the

> To applaud the will of God, to do the will of God, even to fight for the
> will of God is not difficult . . . until it comes at cross-purposes with our
> will. Then the lines are drawn.
>
> —Richard J. Foster, *Christian Reader*

past two years a congregation of a different denomination had
shared the facilities of Community Church, a smaller Los
Angeles congregation. The pastor had taken pity on a group
which needed a place to call home. They had their own set of
keys and were meeting in the buildings even before the
trustees approved it. Ad-hoc became permanent.

Problems multiplied. Clean-up was hit-and-miss. They
would meet at all hours without prior scheduling. Half the
choir robe closet was appropriated without asking. The last
straw was the overwhelming stench of rotting, half-eaten fish
left over from a fellowship dinner. The odor clung to the primary classroom for days. In the confrontation that followed,
the trustee chairman resigned. Though they finally departed,
the host congregation was left scarred and bitter. "Never
again," the pastor told me.[1]

Making the determination to take in a group to share your
church cannot be taken lightly. It is a decision that requires
the leadership and congregation to enter into a prolonged
period of prayer followed by an extensive investigation into
the feasibility and practicality of such an undertaking. Once
your church door has been opened and the guest group is in,
it is extremely difficult to remove them without causing hard
feelings that ripple through both congregations for years to
come.

Paul and Barnabas

An unsettling question that arises when a separation is
inevitable is, Was it God's will that we share the church from
the beginning? To answer this question we refer to the incident that brought about the split up of Paul and Barnabas in

the Book of Acts. Now Barnabas, a Levite from the island of Cyprus and cousin of the evangelist Mark, is described as "a good man and full of the Holy Spirit and faith" (Acts 11:24), traits that gave him influence and leadership. No doubt Barnabas was a tremendous asset to Paul during the first missionary journey that brought them to some of the principal cities of Asia Minor, but a dispute arose as they prepared for a second missionary journey that permanently changed things in their relationship, even to the extent that they parted company. Barnabas went with Mark to Cyprus, while Paul and Silas went through Syria.

Theirs was not a theological dispute, but one, firstly, that centered around Peter's instability toward the Gentiles—clearly a church issue that Paul had to clear up by pronouncing that the gospel was to be to the Jew first, then to the Gentile (Rom. 1:16). And secondly, their dispute centered on Barnabas's desire to include Mark in the team while Paul disagreed, citing his disloyalty at Pamphylia. This dispute could not be reconciled, so Paul asked Barnabas to leave (Acts 15:36–41; Gal. 2:11–14). Despite this separation, they continued to work together in other endeavors for the sake of the gospel (1 Cor. 9:6; 2 Cor. 8:18–19).[2] At this juncture we may ask if it was God's will that Paul and Barnabas join in the first place. Obviously it was. But it was not meant to be a permanent relationship. When it reached the place where they were at cross-purposes with one another, they had to break off their relationship.

If you are sharing your church and have exhausted all the means we have prescribed and find that you, as the host church, are still at cross-purposes with your guest church—the lines being drawn—you are released from the bond that originally brought you together.

Protecting God's Honor

A fundamental reason for dissolving a relationship that has no future is to protect God's honor. The reputation of God is continuously assailed by the unbelieving world, and the last thing opponents of the church need is more ammunition to support their argument. The host church that continues to share its facility with a group that disgraces God, or is antagonistic to the host church's purpose, will undoubtedly cast aspersions on God's glory and the witness of the host church's ministry. The apostle Paul alludes to this truth when he says,

> And then all of us can praise the Lord together with one voice, giving glory to God, the Father of our Lord Jesus Christ. So, warmly welcome each other into the church, just as Christ has warmly welcomed you; then God will be glorified.
>
> Romans 15:6–7 TLB

The teaching here is that as a unified body we praise the Lord, giving glory to God, the counterpoint being that disharmony robs God of glory and honor due his name. The leadership of both the host and guest churches must prevail upon God's wisdom to know when it is time to call it quits, allowing no other consideration to take priority, for the protection of God's honor.

Case in Point

A fellow pastor related to me the following account of the events that led up to his asking their guest groups to leave the church. The host church allowed three different cultural groups, in addition to the American group, to share their facility. The approximate total members in all three guest groups was in excess of 475 persons. One of the groups, described as a Christian organization, was allowed to rent a portion of the facility until they "became a deterrent to the host church." This "deterrent" was reported to be abusing the building, misusing equipment, and generally ceasing to be good housekeepers.

This fellow pastor also cited the reasons he asked the two other groups to leave: (1) The host church needed additional room to grow, and (2) the guest groups outgrew the sanctuary and parking facilities.

Naturally this pastor was committed to protecting God's honor by averting any heightening conflict with this group. But, in addition to that, his concern was to protect his flock of believers who viewed the guest groups as a deterrent to their worship and commitment to their church.

Protecting the Body of Believers

A second reason for bringing a host-guest relationship to an end is to protect the body of believers, the congregations that make up the church. Hostilities can easily emerge between the two groups when it is apparent that the proper concord cannot be reached. Christians are saved *sinners*, fully capable of demonstrating their dislike for each other despite their commitment to the church. If, in their mind, the integrity of their church is threatened after all efforts toward reconciliation have been exhausted, they will react accordingly. This may lead to collateral damage in the host or guest ministry. It is, therefore, the duty of the senior pastors to intervene and to bring about an equitable dissolution in the host-guest relationship before further, possibly irreparable, weakening to the body of Christ can occur.

Case in Point

A brother in the Lord, a fellow pastor and close friend, related another relevant story. A doctrinally sound group occupied a building on a church property for nearly five years before this man was called to be the senior pastor of the host church. This group numbered in excess of one hundred persons and came to use the church building under sponsorship of a nearby sending church. There was no written agreement, and the guest group paid rent that included all their utilities.

Under the leadership of my fellow pastor, the host church experienced significant growth, which signaled the beginning of problems. When both groups were small, the problems seemed to be minimal, but with growth came trouble, especially to the host church.

1. Conflict in schedules between the host and guest groups escalated.
2. The guest group neglected to maintain the overall condition of their section of the facility. This included some destruction of property and an apathetic view toward housekeeping.
3. The children's activities were not properly supervised. This led to defacing of walls and dirty rooms.
4. When the pastor was approached about the deteriorating conditions, he took the problems upon himself instead of involving his congregation and was, therefore, unable to keep up with the maintenance.
5. There was a push for more areas to occupy.

The majority of the leadership of the host church agreed that the relationship should be severed. There were several reasons for this decision: (1) It was costing the host church financially to accommodate the guest group. Since population growth to the host church was restrained by the guest group's presence, this translated into lower budget offerings. (2) The wear and tear on the building represented a significant drop in value due to depreciation of the facility. (3) Cleanup was becoming an increasing problem. These situations, when added to other minor infractions, began to mushroom until the consensus in the leadership was "we would rather see them move on."

Several interesting observations by this pastor should be mentioned. In his view, taking on a guest group to help them get started is the Christian thing to do. But, as he pointed out, "when they are able to sustain themselves, they should move on." Because the guest group, in his words, can become complacent, it is better for them to have the goal of only using the host church as a temporary location.

Protecting the Reputation and Image of Your Church

What people think about your ministry is vitally important to the future of your church. The neighborhood surrounding your church, along with the community at large, is ever vigilant to watch the Christian church to see if indeed Christianity is working. The apostle Paul writes, "You yourselves are our letter, written on our hearts, known and read by everybody" (2 Cor. 3:2). This affirms the truth that the unbelieving world is watching the testimony of the church as well as the individual believer, looking to see how they react in crisis and everyday life. Nonbelievers may not be reading the Bible, but they are reading your life and the life of your church. What message are they getting? One of unity or of discordance?

Other Christian churches, too, are watching those churches that share facilities and monitoring any conflicts to see if the alliance between host and guest churches can be implemented in their own church without a multitude of problems. When the reputation or property of the host church is abused, people talk. Disgruntled congregation members, as well as the public, talk about your "model" church. Often this talk is sprinkled with personal incidents that further promote dissension that can easily circulate into the community.

Every church building in America stands as a silent testimonial to God. Every Christian church is a reminder to society of the atoning work of Christ on the cross. While the church building itself is certainly not the life of the church, that being the vibrant body of Christ, it *is* emblematic of the teachings of the Bible. This is why it is vitally important that the image of the church be protected. This image, which includes the church property, may be the only visible symbol the unchurched see. Adequate measures should be taken by both the host and guest group to uphold this image. When the reputation or image of the host church is threatened by the guest group, this may signal the end of the relationship.

15

Sharing Your Church as a New Pastor

A pastor or candidate who is willing to accept a call to a church that is sharing its facility must be up to the unique challenge that kind of ministry will demand of him. Having a passion for God, along with a holy ambition to serve, will drive the engine of the new pastor to great heights—affording an excellent ministry—and help him accomplish the tasks the unambitious might consider unattainable. This kind of pastor will do well at the church that shares its buildings with other ministries.

When to Move

Knowing when to leave one congregation and move to another to assume responsibilities that include various cultures can be an agonizing decision. From a spiritual perspective, the pastor might be ready to work at this sort of church if he has the following things:

1. He has peace and assurance from the Holy Spirit— God's voice—that this change is from God. This is accomplished through great periods of prayer.
2. He has the assurance from Scripture that this change does not in any way violate the will of God.
3. He has sought out counsel and guidance from godly sources.
4. His spouse and family support the decision whole-heartedly.
5. The new church has extended a call based on a majority vote.
6. The circumstances that prevail upon him are pointing in the direction that favors moving.
7. His personal desires confirm that this move is beneficial.

From a secular perspective, the prospective pastor should know when to move when he admits he is versatile and flexible enough to adapt to change and possesses adequate people skills that will enable him to embrace other cultures.

Considerations in Moving

Some pastors are extremely effective in ministry by staying in one church a long time, while others are the opposite— they diminish in effectiveness over extended durations. Persistent problems in the present church, along with financial difficulties and ministerial exhaustion, can be vital contributors that promote moving to another ministry. But moving to another ministry that is *sharing its church* with other cultures requires special thoughtfulness:

1. Do you like the cultural groups that are sharing the prospective church? Is there any question about the ethnic groups or their characteristics that may limit your leadership or represent a negative factor?
2. Are there other pastors in your network that can share with you their experience with the groups in question?

(Discovering case histories on similar ministries may assist your decision making.)

3. After considering the racial profiles of the groups in the prospective church, are you and your family comfortable with them?

If your prospective church is multi-American (more than one American group; e.g., American Baptist and American Messianic, etc.), that kind of ministry will also require unique talents that may test your faith and ability to work within a multiministry environment. Although the procedures set forth herein are from a Baptist perspective, the fundamental principles still hold regardless of denomination, type of ministry, or relative size.

Candidating

The interviewing process between committee and candidating pastor should disclose sufficient information to enable both parties to discern if each other's expectations can be met in the future. The committee must factor into the equation the candidate's ability to relate to the identity of the multicongregation makeup, while the candidate must evaluate not only the identity of the multicongregation, but the talents, interests, and commitments of the host church membership as well as the neighborhood they serve. The candidating pastor may well ask the chairperson or other committee member some of the questions Douglas Scott suggests:

1. *What has been the most significant event in the life of this congregation since you have been a member?* This question serves two purposes: We discover what events are significant to them and we see what ministries this congregation considers significant.
2. *Aside from the upheaval of looking for a new pastor, what has been the most upsetting event in the life of this church?* While they may have had plenty of private (and

potentially divisive) thoughts and comments before, this question allows them to voice their pain openly. It also allows us the luxury of future vision—knowing what is likely to upset them in the years ahead.

3. *What areas of concern need to be addressed by this congregation?* Delightfully nonspecific, this question may be the perfect invitation for a committee member to open an issue that is unresolved. [1]

This initial discovery period should provide the candidate with vital information that is necessary to build the framework to come to a decision. Questions like the aforementioned should be asked from a multicultural, multicongregational perspective: Was the most significant event in the life of this congregation related to the guest group? Good or bad? Was the most upsetting event in the life of this church related to the guest group? This should give the prospective pastor a representative slice of how the leadership really feels about the guest ministry. If the areas of concern in the congregation revolve around the guest group, this may be a signal to the inquiring pastor that a major problem exists.

Leadership Requirements

A number of passages in Scripture develop leadership requirements that provide guidelines for pastors, namely, Acts 6:1–6, 1 Timothy 3:1–13, 2 Timothy 2:1–13, and Titus 1:5–9. The summation of these passages forms the acronym F-A-I-T-H:

Faithfulness
Ability
Integrity
Trustworthiness
Humility

Faithfulness

Faithfulness on the part of the newly appointed pastor and his staff is akin to commitment. When we are faithful to Christ, honoring him above all else, that dedication will trickle down into our commitment as effective ministers of the gospel. Serving God with passion and obedience is a requisite for leadership. When a pastor demonstrates this in his own life, he can expect it of his staff, deacons, and church family.

Ability

Ability is the capacity of the pastor to effectively discern and navigate in the Scriptures to distinguish when to preach or teach the Word of God. The Word of God must be the central focus in your ministry; everything else is subordinate to it. When we are competent in the Bible, we are able to care for the saint and counsel the sinner. Having a good grasp of the major doctrines that support the progress of redemption from Genesis to Revelation will serve you well as the new pastor. The first task you, as the new pastor, should undertake is to discover what role the Bible plays in the lives of your staff and leadership. This will be an indicator of the importance of the Scriptures in the life of the congregation.

Integrity

Integrity is a personal quality. It is that level of character and fidelity that you have established between you and God. It is an imaginary line of restraint that you agreed on with God in the intimacy of your heart. This line of integrity keeps you from compromise that can lead to spiritual, moral, or ethical failure. On the other side of the line of integrity is the destruction of your ministry, your home, and your witness. This fear should keep you from crossing over.

Trustworthiness

A suitable synonym for trustworthiness is conviction. The apostle Paul advises that a novice or new convert should not be appointed to a leadership position too soon because conviction or trustworthiness takes time to develop. Rick Warren rightly affirms this truth: "Wise leaders understand that people will give mental and verbal assent to what they are told, but they will hold with conviction what they discover for themselves."[2] Our convictions are an integral part of our foundation of faith, and they should be visible in times of crisis and calm.

Humility

"Humility in the spiritual sense is an inwrought grace of the soul that allows one to think of himself no more highly than he ought to think (Eph. 4:1–2; Col. 3:12–13; cf. Rom. 12:3)."[3] In the megachurches of today (and to a lesser extent, in smaller churches), there are many competent pastors who have extensive educational backgrounds, and so it is not uncommon to see postgraduate degrees—both master's and doctorate's—hanging on the pastor's office wall. This, in the life of the spiritual leader, should not contribute to self-aggrandizement. Ministerial experience, too, can contribute to inordinate pride. James addresses this when he teaches: "Humble yourselves before the Lord, and he will lift you up" (James 4:10). Inordinate pride frequently emerges out of success, while humility emerges out of hardship. The spiritual leader should learn from the lessons we find in Scripture, and not from his own personal experience, that excessive pride is harmful.

These leadership requirements are basic and may vary with the individual, because each candidate for the pastorate must evaluate his own personal strengths and weaknesses in light of the task he is asked to undertake.

We are paralyzed by fear of taking risks. "Behold the turtle—he makes
progress only when he sticks his neck out."
                                —James Bryant Conant, president of Harvard[4]

Transitions into a New Ministry

When a pastor makes the change to a church that hosts
other groups, make no mistake about it, it is a calling that
requires special direction and leadership. The goal of the man
whom God is calling should be to move well. That is, to move
with the minimum amount of disruption to his present and
future ministry, as well as his own personal life. Naturally,
there is an element of fear to be dealt with—fear of the future,
the unknown, and, of course, failure.

Fear, even to the Christian, is a real threat, but as Jay
Adams observes, fear need not overtake us because "The
enemy of fear is love; the way to put off fear, then, is to put
on love."[5] Our love for the Lord must dictate to our emotions
that what lies ahead in the providence of God is able to over-
power any fear and that the future is going to be an adventure, one filled with golden opportunities to serve God. The
apostle John writes: "There is no fear in love. But perfect
['mature'] love drives out fear, because fear has to do with
punishment. The one who fears is not made perfect ['mature']
in love" (1 John 4:18). This explains that the perfect or mature
Christian who draws closer to Christ in an intimate "love
affair" with him will see fear flee from his or her heart.

Back in 1987, when the Lord called my wife and me to
leave our ministry, families, home, friends, and employment
in New York and relocate to South Florida to direct a Messianic ministry, a great fear came over my wife, and to a lesser
degree, myself. To leave life and family because of a calling
to an "unknown land" was asking a great deal since it involved
many risks. But my confidence in God was unshaken because
God had told me, in my spirit, that this was from him.

This confidence came about one Sunday as I was preaching on Abraham's calling from God where he was asked to leave the land of his fathers and head south (Gen. 12:9). It suddenly occurred to me that the Lord wanted me to *take more of him,* to head "south" as well. To take a step—a leap?—of faith into the unknown and to just follow him. To this day (almost fifteen years later) there are no regrets by either my wife or myself.

Beginning in Your New Ministry

God promises us an extra measure of grace when we take on a new ministry (2 Cor. 9:8; 12:9; Eph. 3:20; Phil. 4:13), so be sure to apply that "unmerited favor" liberally. The first application must be to start off on the right footing. As Robert Kemper advises:

> We cannot begin at a congregation twice, so we must use this unique opportunity well. If thoughtfully and imaginatively done, the events of the first year set a tone and approach that a pastor and congregation can enjoy for years to come.[6]

When the new pastor takes over a ministry that is sharing its church, how he reacts to that new environment in his initial period is crucial and will set the stage for any future acts.

1. The new host pastor must meet with the guest pastor(s) and his leadership to establish the authority base. The question about who's in charge should be settled early in the new pastor's administration. Reviewing the written resolutions should curtail any disputes by providing a base to build on.
2. The new host pastor must establish a method of getting to know his guest pastor and staff on a level that penetrates beyond their former commitment to the previous pastor. Aspiring to a higher plateau of excellence should be part of the creed of the new pastor's life work.

3. While some changes to the administration and staff, and the facility, need to be implemented immediately, major changes should be postponed for at least one year. This will give the host and guest ministries ample time to investigate the interpersonal relationship between the two groups.

4. Paul writes, "To the Jews I became like a Jew, to win the Jews. . . . I have become all things to all men so that by all possible means I might save some" (1 Cor. 9:20, 22). Paul's mind-set instructs the new pastor to adapt himself to his new environment—the guest culture—for the sake of the gospel.

5. Understandably, some members of the guest group will not take to the new pastor. This is a variable factor that depends on time and favor. In time, these people will realize the new pastor has their interest at heart and will change their view accordingly. When the leadership of the guest church shows favor toward the new host pastor, this too will convey a message of acceptance.

Most people are opposed to change. Whether in ministry or secular work, geographic, lifestyle, or economic change is difficult for mortals. As Mark Twain put it, "The only person who likes change is a wet baby." Yet out of change can come greatness. It all depends on our relationship to God and our spiritual perspective.

16

The Joy of Sharing
Worship Together

The culmination of three months of hard labor on our church buildings came on August 8, 1999, when the Americans and Brazilians shared the joy of worshiping together in their rededication ceremony. This spectacular event was marked by the splendor of joint worship, prayer, and testimony, in remembrance of the wonder of God displayed in our dual-cultural ministry. More than seven hundred people came from surrounding cities and towns to see the God worshiped at North Pompano Baptist Church!

Working together, the Americans and Brazilians cleaned up the buildings and property, painted the walls (inside and outside), replaced furniture and furnishings, and brought a new look to a struggling ministry and neglected facility. Using the talents of the Brazilian music ministry, our worship leader joined forces with them to put on a wonderful presentation in song to honor the Lord. Then the Brazilian pastor and I shared our heartfelt thanks to the Lord through the teaching of the Word of God, and the two brief messages from the Bible brought purpose and fulfillment to the evening.

The celebration reminded me in a small way of the great festival in Israel commemorating the completion and dedication of Solomon's temple. Afterward, the jubilee-like atmosphere continued as the two congregations enjoyed fellowship and food together, reaching across the cultural lines by building bridges that would unite the two groups for years to come.

The Healing Power of Sharing Worship

The joining together of two cultures for worship is not new. Peter experienced a change of heart in this regard in Acts 10–11 when Christ directed him to invite the Gentiles into worship along with the Jewish Christians. This event established the truth that salvation was open to all who would believe in Christ. This momentous incident was also a milestone in the healing process between the Jew and Gentile. Because Jesus the Messiah had broken down the wall between the two, they could now heal their relationship by sharing their faith in Christ together.

What Christ accomplished in the Book of Acts, he purposes to accomplish in the church today through the operation of the Holy Spirit.

> Consequently, you are no longer foreigners and aliens, but fellow citizens with God's people and members of God's household, built on the foundation of the apostles and prophets, with Christ Jesus himself as the chief cornerstone. *In him the whole building is joined together and rises to become a holy temple in the Lord.*
>
> Ephesians 2:19–22, italics mine

Today, God is using the opportunity of joint worship as a method of healing differences between cultures, and between individuals as well. Cultural problems have been with us since the time of Isaac and Ishmael, and it is certain they will remain until Christ returns. This is why the church must set the example when it comes to providing a "balm in Gilead"

to the hurting world, and must show them that Christ is concerned with all their needs.

We, the church, are the whole building that is joined
together. If we cannot make healing work in the church, we
dare not try to export our Christianity to an unbelieving world
that will only criticize the work of God accordingly. We have
a hurting society today that is crying out in pain, and the
church must stand as a sentinel of the truth that unity in
Christ does indeed exist and it is a healing agent for our land.[1]

The Witness of Sharing Worship

Robert Saucy writes, "The church is the place where the
new life of Christ in the Spirit is manifest. The gospel reconciles man to God but also reconciles man to man. The evidence of this reality in the church is a witness to the world."[2]
Saucy embraces the truth that reconciliation, when exhib-
ited in the church—especially between divergent cultures—
is a dynamic witness to the unbelieving world that is dra-
matically demonstrated in the act of corporate worship. There
is no reason why both host and guest groups cannot come
together for corporate worship under one Spirit. We should
be able to set aside any misgivings toward one another to proclaim our witness to the public.

Paul says this is possible under any circumstance:

> Christ . . . gave us the ministry of reconciliation: that God was
> reconciling the world to himself in Christ, not counting men's
> sins against them. And he has committed to us the message
> of reconciliation. We are therefore Christ's ambassadors, as
> though God were making his appeal through us.
>
> 2 Corinthians 5:18–20

Reconciling the world to himself most certainly includes the
corporate worship of God by different cultures regardless of
any situations that would prohibit it.

How to Share Worship

How an individual worships God is his or her own private concern, based on his or her personal relationship with the Creator. Many Christians are able to worship God at home, in their prayer closet, or perhaps in their bathroom. We are told that the surrendered life to Christ in itself is an act of worship (Rom. 12:1). Others enjoy worship in a sanctuary filled with God's people as a public display of God's presence. Music, song, praise, and testimonials to God are all legitimate forms of worship that prepare the heart and spirit to embrace the written word that supplies us with spiritual nourishment. Regardless of your private or public choice to meet with God in worship, your experience can only be deepened when you share your worship with other cultures regularly or intermittently. To meet with God as a mixed group of both host and guest church together is in a small way a glimpse of what lies ahead for us in heaven.

The Example of the Great Multitude

The prophetic Book of Revelation gives the Christian a preview of what to expect when we leave this world to dwell in heaven with God:

After this I heard what sounded like the roar of a great multitude in heaven shouting:

"Hallelujah!
Salvation and glory and power belong to our God,
    for true and just are his judgments. . . ."
And again they shouted:

"Hallelujah! . . ."

The twenty-four elders and the four living creatures fell down and worshiped God, who was seated on the throne. And they cried:

"Amen, Hallelujah!"

Then a voice came from the throne, saying:

"Praise our God,
   all you his servants,
you who fear him,
   both small and great!"

Then I heard what sounded like a great multitude, like the
roar of rushing waters and like loud peals of thunder, shouting:

"Hallelujah!
   For our Lord God Almighty reigns.
Let us rejoice and be glad
   and give him glory!
For the wedding of the Lamb has come,
   and his bride has made herself ready.
Fine linen, bright and clean,
   was given her to wear."

Revelation 19:1–8

This worship service during the marriage ceremony of the
Lamb is going to be awesome! This great, mixed multitude
includes every nationality represented on earth as well as all
the angels and heavenly elders (Rev. 7:11, 13). This tells us
that any sharing church on earth that embraces other cultures and holds corporate worship is simply practicing for
that which is to come in heaven. There will be shouting, the
falling down and worshiping at Christ's feet, rejoicing, glad-
ness, and the divine unity of humanity that comes through
sharing worship.

While it is comforting to envision what corporate worship
is going to be like in heaven, it is practical to develop a plan
of how to engage in that kind of worship while we're still on
earth.

Allow the Holy Spirit to Initiate and Reign

To avoid a circuslike worship service, it is better to allow
God's Spirit to speak to the hearts of both the host and guest

For much that is undertaken by the Church He [the Holy Spirit] is not necessary. The Holy Ghost is no more needed to run bazaars, social clubs, institutions, and picnics, than He is to run a circus. When the Church is run on the same lines as a circus, there may be crowds, but there is no Shekinah.

—Samuel Chadwick, *The Way to Pentecost*[3]

pastors to bring such an undertaking together. The Holy Spirit knows when the time is right to begin sharing your worship service with your guest group, so don't rush it. Be mindful of the fact that God is superintending all the events at your church, and many elements need to be taken into consideration before a corporate worship service can be held. While you may be concerned with the ability, even the failures and shortcomings, of both congregations to bring such an event together, God is more concerned with the heart attitude of all the people involved. Jim Cymbala notes,

> The Holy Spirit is still greater today than all our shortcom-ings and failures. He has come to free us from the restraints and complexes of insufficient talent, intelligence, or upbring-ing. He intends to do through us what only he can do. The issue is not our *ability* but rather our *availability* to the per-son of the Holy Spirit.[4]

The key issue here is whether or not both congregations really want to share in corporate worship. They may be *able*, but are they *available* to the Holy Spirit? God's Spirit craves to bring cohesiveness to the ministry and to enrich the wor-ship experience. His plan is to do this through the medium of Christian unity. That unity is achieved when any walls of prej-udice or cultural intolerance have been dismantled. That unity is further achieved when any notion of superiority is removed. When we are clear of these obstacles and see each other as one, we are available to the person of the Holy Spirit. Then, if the Holy Spirit has prompted the leadership of both congregations to discuss sharing worship, you have the confidence that this movement is from God.

Establish a Sharing Program

When both pastors and their leadership meet to discuss sharing worship, agreeing on their concept of God and commensurate kinds of worship must be central to the discussion. Charles Colson quotes Spinoza, who affirmed this when he said, "Man builds his kingdoms in accordance with his concept of God."[5] This key element should be foundational and should set the agenda for your program. The host group's concept of worship may be radically different from that of the guest group, and while diversity can be good in some cases, confusion is not good. The program will stay on track if you build it on the proper concept of God, one that you both agree on.

Part of establishing a program is scheduling. There are four aspects of scheduling: dates, events, preachers, and creativity.

Dates: The leadership (pastors and deacons or elders) needs to decide how frequently the worship service is to be shared. Some churches may decide to conduct joint worship services every week. Others may choose to share worship on a quarterly basis. Experience may determine what interval works best for your church. Caution would dictate that before any commitment is made to regularly join services, a trial and error period should be introduced.

Events: Special Christian events such as Christmas, Easter, and Passover provide excellent opportunities to inaugurate a corporate worship service. With varied cultures and their approach to the holiday providing an interesting backdrop to the occasion, the joint worship service should be a fulfilling experience. Other congregational ceremonial events such as communion and baptism can certainly complement a joint worship service.

Preachers: Scheduling which pastor is to preach at the joint service is a matter for the pastors themselves to agree on. Rotating the pastors seems to be the best method in order to

---

Creativity causes people to think about what they're doing.
—Jim Rose, quoted in *Leadership,* vol. 14, no. 3

---

avoid redundancy and complacency. Naturally, the host congregation hears the host pastor preach each Sunday, as does the guest congregation hear their pastor preach each Sunday, so to rotate would refresh the spirits of everyone concerned. Occasionally, both pastors may preach consecutively, but this should not be a standing rule.

Creativity: Allowing God's Spirit to move freely will promote creativity—a much-needed quality when a church shares its worship service. A key ingredient in the creativity process is nonconformity. Corporate worship is not your standard form of worship; therefore few textbooks are available for reference and few church pastors are available for consultation. This gives the sharing church great latitude to create its own form of corporate worship that works best for them. This creativity may influence the worship music, singing, and other elements of the worship service, such as the way the tithes and offerings are collected.

Organize Teams

The host and guest group should appoint a ministry head or captain to direct the various teams necessary to conduct a successful corporate worship service. The captain of the team will also function as the liaison between the host and guest groups to arrange the facility availability, the dates of the practices (for the worship ministry), cleanup, and food preparation, if any. Additional teams will also be needed to handle the offering and the invitation response. Protocol involving the worship choir and praise teams should come from the host and guest groups' music ministers.

Avoid the Bells and Whistles

Several years ago, I was attending a Sunday service at a nearby church that turned to a progressive style of worship.

After the congregation and visitors were seated, they closed the outside doors and a quieting hush came over the audience as their attention was directed toward the stage area at the front of the sanctuary. Then a singing voice came over the sound system and heads turned to the rear of the church only to find the music minister walking toward the altar area holding a wireless microphone, belting out a hymn as if he were walking down a runway on Broadway. From there, things became more progressive.

The music director ended his hymn on the stage as the church's gospel drama club began to act out a scene that related to the sermon. For the next thirteen *long* minutes we watched various members perform their hearts out, props and all, to prepare the congregation/audience for the Word of God.

Now what is wrong with this picture? When the church has to resort to secular methods that border on sensationalism to hold the interest of congregations, we are in trouble. Not only does it diminish the impact of the sermon, but it promotes competition between the actors vying for the best parts week after week. If the Word of God isn't enough to bring the people in and challenge them to a greater commitment to Christ, then what are we going to do next year to entertain after the thrill of drama wears off? Bring in rock bands? Psychedelic lights perhaps? Serve popcorn?

It's important, therefore, to avoid "fireworks." Foreseeing this as a real problem that will invade the church in the future, Samuel Chadwick observed,

> Stage-lights have found their way into the Church. The red glare dazzles, but it does not burn. Fireworks are brilliant, but they end with the hour. No ideals are kindled, no ministry impelled, no sacrifice inspired. The pretense of spirituality is the worst profanity.[6]

Chadwick's point throughout his exemplary work *The Way to Pentecost* is that the way to find direction for our worship is to extol the name of Christ and to seek fellowship with his

Spirit. That's it. We don't need the bells and whistles to attract the crowds if we are really in tune with God and open to the leading of his Spirit. God's Spirit will do the work! In my estimation, the "fireworks" actually take away from the impact and effectiveness of the sermon by glamorizing it with pretty wrappings, ribbons, and bows. God's glory cannot be diminished and, therefore, the fireworks are simply not needed.

When sharing a worship service, there is often a tendency for the combined groups to overdo it. This may be due in part to trying to surpass and outmatch each other. The host and guest pastors or deacons should monitor the leadership team to prevent this from interfering with the overall spirit of sharing the service.

It's also helpful to avoid the use of "gadgets." When we discuss gadgets, we are not talking about trinkets or souvenirs that are distributed by the ushers to members and guests as they enter or leave the church. No, gadgets in this context would be of a different variety. A constant diet of celebrity speakers to fill the pulpit would be a kind of gadget that is used to entice people to worship. Cannot the Holy Spirit accomplish this for the praying congregation? Another form of gadget is an infusion of Christian rock singers or bands, which in many ways imitate secular artists. And then there is extraordinary advertising. Some churches have a large percentage of their annual budget designated for event advertising, which oftentimes fails to produce the desired results. Waiting on the Spirit may prove to be a profitable alternative.

Jim Cymbala knows firsthand that when it comes to bringing people into his church to worship God, gadgets don't work. As the senior pastor of the mightily-used-of-the-Lord Brooklyn Tabernacle, his testimony to the power of God's Spirit working in his ministry is unparalleled. He writes:

> The Old Testament declaration is still 100 percent true today: It is "'not by might nor by power, but by my Spirit,' says the Lord Almighty" (Zech. 4:6). A decade of gadgets and gimmicks

will never accomplish what God the Holy Spirit can do in one month as he works in the life of the church.[7]

Case in Point

The worship experience should be the pinnacle of the Christian faith. It should be designed to bring the heart, soul, and spirit to that place where we meet with God. It should strengthen our commitment to both Christ and our ministry, as well as provide a refuge for the weary servant. As many pastors will attest, often that weary servant is the pastor himself.

Building on our position at NPBC of sharing worship, I recently asked the Brazilian pastor to bring us a challenging message for our main Sunday service. He readily agreed, and when the date arrived, he brought his wife to translate Portuguese into English.[8] The pastor entitled his sermon "Building a Life of Commitment" and chose for his text 2 Chronicles 16:9, which reads, "For the eyes of the LORD range throughout the earth to strengthen those whose hearts are fully committed to him." Ordinarily, when one speaks through a translator, a great deal of the meaning can be lost or misinterpreted, diminishing the dynamics of the speaker—but that was not the case here! His wife, a Brazilian who has lived in the United States for many years, speaks excellent English and translated almost simultaneously. Rather than weakening the thrust of the delivery, the rapid translating actually heightened our expectation as we anxiously awaited every word.

The Spirit of God knew exactly what our people needed to hear that day. Every person in the congregation came forward to renew his or her commitment to the Lord. What a sharing experience! As for me, I reveled in the truth as I reminded myself of C. S. Lewis's words, "A man can't always be defending the truth; there must be time to feed on it."[9]

17

Making a Statement in Your Community

Once you become a sharing church, your message to your community will be noticeably different. In our world today, people need to know that God has provided a place where they can find refuge from their trials and troubles in an atmosphere permeated by love. Your neighbors will quickly recognize that sharing is one of the greatest expressions of love, and because you share your church, you are a loving church. This reputation of being a loving church will go a long way in promoting the Great Commission in your community. Mother Teresa made an interesting observation regarding the world's great need for love:

> The greatest disease in the West today is not TB or leprosy; it is being unwanted, unloved, and uncared for. We can cure physical diseases with medicine but the only cure for loneliness, despair, and hopelessness is love. There are many in the world who are dying for a piece of bread but there are many more dying for a little love. The poverty in the West is a different kind of poverty—it is not only poverty of loneliness but

also of spirituality. There's a hunger for love, as there is a hunger for God.[1]

The human spirit longs to have this hunger satisfied. But instead of seeking to satiate its hunger through the things of God or God's love, the world, much to its dissatisfaction, is filling this void with various forms of atheism, agnosticism, spiritualism, materialism, narcissism, hedonism, and many other "isms." In view of this modern trend, the church must rise to the challenge of winning back the human heart and spirit to God by sharing his love that was demonstrated by Christ's death on the cross.

Paul embraces this theme in his letter to Philemon:

> Grace to you and peace from God our Father and the Lord Jesus Christ. I always thank my God as I remember you in my prayers, because I hear about your faith in the Lord Jesus and your love for all the saints. I pray that you may be active in sharing your faith, so that you will have a full understanding of every good thing we have in Christ. Your love has given me great joy and encouragement, because you, brother, have refreshed the hearts of the saints.
>
> Philemon 3–7

The passage clearly encourages the Christian to have the heart of an evangelist and share his or her faith. But I believe the text goes beyond the obvious to inseparably link *love* with *sharing*. Knowing that love is one of the basic human needs, and that sharing is an extension of this love, the church must realign its approach to reach its community.

Why Do People Attend Church?

In a recent article, Ralph Wilson suggests several reasons why people attend church.[2] Among them are

1. Social standing
2. Networking for business

3. Looking for a future husband or wife
4. Family tradition
5. The responsibility to raise their children with religion
6. Personal growth
7. The need for significance
8. In the case of teenagers, to get away from difficulties at home or to find a boy/girlfriend

Weightier, more pertinent reasons include:

1. Coming to know who God is
2. People are hurting, and they need healing in God
3. Friendship: the desire to build relationships in a community

We agree there are various reasons people attend church, many for purposes that are not too pleasing to God. Nevertheless, God can and often does use man's fallacious reasoning to bring people to himself. The common denominator in the list of why people attend church can be summed up in two sentences: People are searching for love to heal their hurts. God can use the sharing spirit in the church community to meet that need. The message seems to be, "If I go to church, God can meet me there." As Blaise Pascal said, "There's a God-shaped vacuum in every man that only God can fill."

When a congregation shares its church, it is making the public statement that it is willing to risk loving other groups as a witness to its faith in Christ. Naturally, one would conclude that if that church can risk loving another group (be it American or another culture), that church would not hesitate to embrace a wounded individual in need of healing. This is Christ's message and the mission of his church.

The Modern Trend of Isolationism

The trend in our present-day society is a form of isolationism. People want to be left alone. They don't want to get involved with other people. They want to live in gated communities away from the outside world. They want their homes to be their own little fortresses, with security fences and video surveillance systems to protect their privacy. They want a vast expanse between their home and their neighbor to ensure seclusion. Telephone answering machines make isolationism even more apparent; they don't even want to answer their phones unless caller ID shows them who is calling.

But when a crisis comes upon them, they are suddenly willing to forfeit their privacy; they want the community to rally around them for healing. Many, as the Scriptures claim, cry out to God in their misery and affliction (see Hosea 5:15). Perhaps the church is partly to blame for this dilemma. Certainly, many of the unchurched have been disillusioned with Christianity due to the misinformation of cults masquerading as Christian organizations or the immorality on the part of church leaders, or the outrageous mismanagement of church funds. Individuals too, claiming to be Christians, have tarnished the name of Christ by their compromising behavior.

But despite these ever-present problems, there are great numbers who are going against the trends of society and are looking to follow after Jesus. This is where the sharing church must step up to the plate, to help others keep their commitments to the work of Christ. When your community sees both the host and the guest group working together in a hope-filled, nonjudgmental environment that honors Christ, they sense the church is healthy and has the potential to fill the God-shaped void in their lives that the world has failed to satisfy.

Community-Minded

The notable Christian theologian Francis A. Schaeffer made a very prophetic statement when he said, "I am convinced that in the twentieth century people all over the world will not listen if we have the right doctrine, the right policy, but are not exhibiting community."[3] Community, as defined in the ecclesiastical sense, is a group that leads a common spiritual life according to a certain church order, sharing common characteristics or interests, distinct from the larger society within which it exists. For our purposes, the sharing of your church will exhibit *community* to your community.

People in the community are watching the church that shares its facility to see if Christianity really works, if unity really works. They're watching to see if the community system they observe in the church is better than their life of isolation at home.

Outside, Looking In

At NPBC, the outside of our church is a representative slice of what one may expect to see on the inside. On a typical Sunday morning around the time our worship services are to begin, there are multitudes of people busily moving around our buildings. There are scores of Americans, Brazilians, and Haitians parking cars, walking up to the sanctuary or Sunday school class, sitting and talking on the outside benches, preparing the after-service fellowship luncheon—all working together to make the worship experience what God wants it to be. This is the picture we present to the community at large, that we are a sharing community of Christians.

Missionary-Minded

The Christian missionary has been commissioned by God and sent by a particular church to carry on evangelism activities to a designated community, with the purpose of persuading or converting them to his or her beliefs. This challenge is being acted out locally when a congregation shares their church with others; it is the implementation of their mission statement. The blaring proclamation your sharing church will make to the community is that you are missionary-minded because you are equipping your congregation for mission work by teaching them about other cultures right here at home in your own church.

God *Is* Relevant

When people live as if there is no God, we can generally dispute their argument for atheism using apologetic methods. But when they live as if there is indeed a God, but that God is insignificant or that his existence doesn't matter to them, society has arrived at a very dangerous place. This form of heresy is an entrenched enemy that is currently attacking the fundamentals of our faith. For the church not to protect itself against this peril is to ignore our responsibility to defend the Bible and the cause of Christ.

The irrelevancy of God is a concept that emerged out of the thinking of a German philosopher, Friedrich Nietzsche. Nietzsche believed that man would reach a plateau in time when he would live as if God didn't matter. Charles Colson explains:

> In 1889 Friedrich Nietzsche told a parable. . . . Nietzsche's point was not that God does not exist, but that God has become irrelevant. Men and women may assert that God exists or that He does not, but it makes little difference either way. God is dead not because He doesn't exist, but because we live, play, procreate, govern, and die as though He doesn't.[4]

The modern church can combat this thinking by making a statement to the searching and observing community by being unified and sharing that God is relevant. Sharing is a vibrant example to the unbelieving world that God exists and that he matters. This relevancy issue has plenty to do with how people respond to the church in their community. When they see a united church community in action, they conclude that God is very much alive because he is significant in the lives of his people.

18

The Future Outlook of the American Church

Many marketing analysts as well as church profilers rely heavily on surveys and statistics. Statistics can act as a gauge that assists in determining market trends and societal priorities that sway future purchasing or even alter the flow of church members, which can influence the direction a ministry should go. Several disturbing statistics that emerged out of a recent Barna Research[1] study may point to why the church today is having a difficult time winning souls to Christ:

1. Ninety-one percent of adults list having good physical health as their top priority in life, making this the highest-rated priority of all.
2. Other priorities listed by at least three out of four adults include living with a high degree of integrity, having one marriage partner for life, having close friends, and having a clear purpose for living.
3. Seven out of ten adults say having a close, personal relationship with God is a top priority.
4. Only half of all adults (53 percent) identify being deeply committed to the Christian faith as a top priority.

5. Less than half of all adults (42 percent) say being active in a local church is one of their top goals in life.
6. Over half of Americans (58 percent) believe that it is more important to please God than to achieve success or win acceptance from other people.
7. Only half of adults who attend Christian churches (51 percent) agree that revival is the top challenge facing the church.
8. By 2010 we will probably have 10 percent to 20 percent of the population relying primarily or exclusively on the Internet for its religious input.[2]

While some of these figures may seem encouraging (7 out of 10 believe a personal relationship with Christ is a top priority, 53 percent are deeply committed to the Christian faith, and 58 percent believe it is more important to please God), the overall survey figures do suggest that many Americans are more concerned with their own physical and social welfare than they are with winning souls to Christ. The burden for the lost and the teaching of the Great Commission are conspicuously absent from this cross section of Americans represented in these studies.

Another study from a different source seems to indicate a similar mind-set on the part of the nation. An excerpt from the study reads:

> We asked one group to define what they felt were the probable or most likely roles of the church in rural culture in the next ten years. The first of the top three roles (of seven defined) is faith gathering. We expected this role. Faithful people gather for worship, to celebrate the sacraments, and to be together in the many ways the Christian traditions transmitted from generation to generation. The second is nurture or care. This includes planned, and even unplanned, relationships in which the church shares in common life experiences. Leadership is caring in whatever form it takes within church and community. The final role is social gathering. The church not only provides meeting spaces in communities, but also claims to be a key location for face-to-face relationships in a town or

village. . . . Community building is described in terms of addressing the needs of the wider society, cooperation with other community groups, and willingness to address local and regional issues. . . . This shift to community building confirms an emerging paradigm of how to be and to do church. The church's faith, its capacity to offer nurture and care is "in order to" serve the whole people of God. . . . Reinventing the congregation means that the congregation no longer sees itself as a place of retreat or withdrawal from its culture.[3]

While these roles are certainly noble in the cause of Christ, the attempt described here to promote community, at least in the sense that Francis Schaeffer meant it, once again falls short of the goal of the Great Commission. When it comes to the kingdom of God, we can only promote the spirit of community when we are active in reaching the community for Christ. Biblically speaking, there simply cannot be any other reason. Hopefully, out of this social thrust into the neighborhood will come the worship of God and the nurture of his people, but the purpose of the church is to reach the unsaved with the gospel. Any other cause may serve the needs of the congregation but diminishes the spirit of the Great Commission.

Americans Describe Their Ideal Church

In the October 1998 article by Barna Research Online entitled "Americans Describe Their Ideal Church," Barna writes in the column "What Really Matters":

Easily the three most significant factors were the beliefs and doctrine of the church, how much the people in the church seem to care about each other, and the quality of the sermons. A majority of the church-goers listed each of these factors as "extremely important."

The other three items that are the highest priority for church shoppers are friendliness to visitors, involvement in serving the poor and disadvantaged, and the quality of programs and classrooms for children. Roughly 45 percent of adult church-goers identified each of these elements as "extremely important."[4]

Because the future of the American church is inseparably linked to the Great Commission, the question that arises from reviewing these surveys is, Where are the evangelical outreach programs? If the desire for national revival remains on or near 51 percent, then we as a church are failing in our task because we are not serious about spreading the Good News of salvation.

The sharing of your church with other Americans or a group of a different culture is simply the outworking of your view of the Great Commission. Let it be said that this is not the only way, but a fulfilling way to meet the mandate.

Where Is the Holy Spirit?

In today's church, there is an upsetting correlation found in the hesitancy toward outreach programs and the minimal reliance on the Holy Spirit for direction in ministry. Jim Cymbala observes:

> Part of our problem is that we have developed a religious industry whose machinery runs smoothly without any need of the Holy Spirit. A. W. Tozer once commented that if God were to take the Holy Spirit out of this world, most of what the church is doing would go right on, and nobody would know the difference.[5]

Both Cymbala and Tozer agree that the modern church (be it in traditional or contemporary format) seems to be missing something. To say that it is the Holy Spirit would be offensive, but can we say that the Holy Spirit does not appear to have dominion over the church and its programs? When we recall Christ's promise of the Holy Spirit in John 16:8, it does remind us once again as to what the purpose of the church is to be: "When he [the Holy Spirit] comes, he will convict the world of guilt in regard to sin and righteousness and judgment."

This points us to Christ's chief concern—seeing souls saved into the kingdom of God through the instrumentality of the Holy Spirit. We can readily say then that the operation of the Holy Spirit is to prepare the hearts of men for the precious invitation to receive Christ as Savior. Once he has prepared them, the Holy Spirit enlightens their spirits to the dire need to receive Christ, and through their act of confession and repentance, salvation is accomplished. Thus, since Christ's priority was to reach the lost, that must be the priority of the church.

This truth is further supported in the great missionary journal, the Book of Acts, where Christ instructed, "But you will receive power when the Holy Spirit comes on you; and you will be my witnesses in Jerusalem, and in all Judea and Samaria, and to the ends of the earth" (Acts 1:8). Not only does this verse supply us with the outline of Acts, but it makes it clear that the Holy Spirit will empower the church to be a witness attesting to Christ's salvation to the entire world. When we bring our church methodology in line with the message of Acts, we will see a great resurgence toward winning souls to Christ.

Is Your Church Homogeneous or Heterogeneous?

Peter Wagner, in his article entitled "The Homogeneous Unit Principle," asserts, "If any truly heterogeneous churches in America are growing, they are exceptions to the rule." "Heterogeneous" in this context means "those churches that include outside groups." In contrast, he maintains that Christians prefer to remain homogeneous, in that they prefer to worship with their own kind. He quotes the missiologist and church growth pioneer Donald McGavran as saying, "People like to become Christians without crossing racial, linguistic, or class barriers."[6]

While the Great Commission directs us to "go therefore and make disciples of all nations" (Matt. 28:19), surveys in today's church consistently show that growth is limited to homogeneous groups. This indicates that culturally hetero-geneous congregations are very rare. Wagner's study adds, "Research within America indicates that most Christian peo-ple meet together for worship and fellowship within the basic sociological groupings into which they are born." However, simply because there is a tendency for American churches to be culturally homogeneous does not mean they should remain as such. On the contrary, for the church to experience the fullness of worship as God intended it to be according to the Great Commission, there must be some degree of het-erogeneity in the congregation.

Racism and prejudice have no place in the church. The experience of sharing your church with other cultures will not only advance the directive of the Great Commission but will also promote goodwill in the community, and it will have a positive effect on your congregation because it encourages interaction with other ethnic groups.

Finally, while it is argued that heterogeneous groups expe-rience curtailed evangelistic potential, the challenge for the modern American church is to discover ways to cross racial and cultural barriers while maintaining the proper evangel-istic potential. (Peter Wagner suggests that few Christians from outside the congregation are likely to be attracted to such a different community.)

Influx of Immigrants

America is currently experiencing an unprecedented num-ber of immigrants from other lands. Along with these immi-grants comes their religion. In South Florida, the Brazilian population alone has reached over 280,000 as of 2001. Whereas most Brazilians are from a Christian heritage, many other immigrants are not. Whereas at one time Muslims, Bud-dhists, Hindus, and others were considered by American

Christian standards to be abstract religious followers who had little or no effect on our lives and our culture, they are now our neighbors, coworkers, and, much to our chagrin, missionaries of their faith in our Christian country. This should alarm the Bible-believing community into serious Christianity.

Sharing your faith and sharing your church are forms of serious Christianity. Charles Colson wrote in *Kingdoms in Conflict* that "A private faith that does not act in the face of oppression is no faith at all."[7] It's serious because it takes chances and risks to advance the cause of Christ in the face of opposition—the very impetus that forged the first-century church. With the tremendous influx of non-Christians into the United States, the church stands the risk of being weakened through assimilation from forces that do not honor the God of the Bible, the God of Israel. This, in time, will present a serious problem to the church. Accordingly, the need for the American church to bond together with other cultures of like faith will do wonders to solidify a front to reach the unchurched[8] for Christ. With one out of three adults (33 percent) being unchurched, with that proportion representing 65 to 70 million adults in America (2000), and roughly 10 million born-again Christians being unchurched,[9] the challenge for the committed Christian to stay active in evangelism is enormous.

Relational Strategy

Reaching the unchurched for Christ is the greatest challenge facing American churches today.

Barna provokes the church to discover the proper approach to this undertaking by presenting his own precept that may indeed help to answer this challenge:

> Churches . . . are experiencing tremendous success at relating to the unchurched. However, there is not a standard formula or program that invariably works among the un-

churched. Getting to know them intimately and then design-
ing relational strategies around their needs and aspirations
makes all the difference.[10]

As I stated before, sharing your church is a relational strategy that will make the difference in your community. Sharing is true Christianity in action, an attribute of the church
that cannot be denied by the unbelieving world.

United We Stand

Our God is a God of unity as seen in his revelation of the
Trinity—God the Father, God the Son, and God the Holy
Spirit. These three often operate independently from one
another, yet agree as one to proclaim the greatness of God.
This, also, is God's plan for his church, that they would be
independent, yet agree as one—to proclaim the greatness of
God. Sharing your church is a giant step in this direction. If
God is calling you to share your church, you are embarking
on a journey that will epitomize Christ's plan for his follow-
ers, and your rewards will be out of this world.

19

Frequently Asked Questions

To afford an opportunity for pastors, the host church, and the guest church to ask questions, we will divide this chapter into those respective categories.

The Host Church Pastor

1. As a newly ordained minister called to an established church that shares with multicultural groups, what should be my immediate concern?

   This question is addressed in chapter 15. Your fundamental concern should be to quickly orient yourself into ministering to the host group to which you were called. For the first sixty days, your sole responsibility is to bring a fresh supply of love, understanding, and stability to the host congregation. After this introductory period you should branch out and embrace any issues that may have developed regarding the guest group(s).

2. I have been approached by a Christian group to share my church, but I know their denomination teaches a different theology from ours. What should I do?

Before making a decision to share your church under these circumstances, you should meet with your elected board or church council and explain the potential areas of difficulty your church may encounter by embracing a group whose theological foundations are dissimilar. This issue is discussed further in chapter 2.

3. I have been asked to share our church by a Christian group that has the reputation of abusing the host facility property and creating problems with the host congregation. What should I do?

After you have interviewed the proposed group's former host pastor, you should meet with the proposed guest pastor and his leadership to discuss any negative reports that have emerged from the group's prior relationship with a host church. Be sure to address the issues from an unbiased position and give the proposed group leadership an opportunity to defend themselves against the allegations and to present any plan they may have to remedy them. Once this is accomplished and your leadership along with the congregation is in *total* agreement, you can proceed with the plan, believing this consensus is from the Lord.

4. A candidating guest group is asking for a lease, but I am reluctant to sign a document to commit our church to a relationship that may compromise our ministry in the future. Is that a lack of faith?

It is not unusual to exercise caution when approaching the subject of sharing your church, especially for the first time. It is not your faith in God that is being exercised when carefully evaluating the potential of sharing your church, but the frailties of men. I would recommend a trial period of perhaps 60 to 180 days in which the host and guest churches determine whether the union will be a good fit. After this trial period you may consider progressing toward lease approval.

5. How do I determine how much to charge the guest group for rent when they share our church?

There are various methods that are described in chapter 8 that will help you in arriving at the proper amount of rent. Among these are step-up, percentage, proportionate, and split arrangements.

6. Many of our veteran members are uneasy about sharing our church, citing that our original constitution had no such provision to introduce other groups into our church facility. How can I persuade them that we should share our church despite this negativity?

Common reason dictates that societal changes demand ecclesiastical changes. Despite attempts to hold on to ultradenominational positions that may be antiquated and frown on changes, the kingdom of God is not static but continuously unfolding. This requires church leadership to take the initiative and encourage the veteran Christians to be open to change by embracing the possibility that God is leading in the direction of sharing your church for the benefit of advancing the plan of God.

7. Our guest group has abused our church. Will I be branded a heel by our congregation and others by asking them to leave?

This issue is discussed in chapter 14. The major thrust of this chapter is essentially to protect your church. Not every marriage between two groups that share a church is from God. Chapter 14 describes various scenarios that may lead to asking your guests to depart.

8. My church is nondenominational. Would the principles described in this book help our leadership to decide on sharing our church?

Adequate measures have been taken throughout this book to maintain the policy that the principles described herein can be applied to any Christian denomination. This theme is elaborated on in chapters 1 and 2.

9. I'm concerned about what our neighboring community will think and do if we bring in an ethnically different group. How do I know if it's the right thing to do for our church and community?

Basically, if the plan is of God, he will bless it and bring it to fruition. Most communities are averse to change, so the introduction of anything foreign, especially if it is religious in nature, is going to be met with resistance. It has been my experience, however, that while the neighborhood community may initially object to the presence of an ethnic group, in time they will accept the host and guest church combination provided there is no immediate threat to their faith and safety. In other words, if a cult organization were to move in, the community would most likely react unfavorably.

10. At what point in the planning stage to share our church should I bring the congregation into the forum?

Once the leadership (your elected or deacon board; church council) unanimously agrees with the proposal and adequate prayer has been applied, the congregation should be informed. If congregational approval is required by your constitution, once the leadership agrees, the congregational vote should be taken.

The Host Church Membership

1. We have heard reports from other churches that guest groups start out friendly and contained, but in time they become arrogant and begin to spread out and take over. Should we be concerned about this when thinking of sharing our church?

Unfortunately, this kind of problem can happen when the guest church begins to grow in numbers. However, much can be accomplished to circumvent this from reaching the point of crisis (refer to chapter 3). The host and guest pastors must agree to some form of Operations Covenant (described in chapter 8) that will place limitations on the guest group as well as insisting on common courtesies to be observed between the two groups.

2. Our guest group has grown larger than our host church. Should we be concerned with this?

Once the guest group grows beyond the size of the host group (assuming there are no other agreements in place to prohibit otherwise), the time may have come to have them look for or construct their own building. If the host church is still of a mind to embrace another guest group, this may give them an opportunity to do so.

3. How much space should we let them have?

The answer to this question depends on a number of factors: (1) How big the guest group is, (2) How much space you can afford to give over to them without sacrificing the effective operation of the host church, and (3) How much space the guests can afford to rent. Once these questions are answered, the host church should be able to determine how much space to let the guest group occupy.

4. How will their ministry affect our worship service?

This depends on the size and availability of the host facility. If the host facility is large enough to afford the guest ministry their own building and that building enables them to set up their own sanctuary, there will be no impact on the host church. But if not, then the host and guest church must arrange alternate times to use the sanctuary. In any case, the host church should have availability to worship as they desire—it is their building.

5. Will the language barrier between the host and guest groups affect our unity?

Most ethnic or foreign groups that have been in America for any length of time have many in their congregation who speak very good English. Normally these people are called to translate so that the operation of the church can function without interruption. I have found that most of the leadership is able to speak fluent English, and there was little or no language barrier with the two different languages at our church. A great deal of the communication is through body language (smiles, frowns, hand motions, and gestures), which is universal.

6. Will our pastor take vital time and effort away from us in order to administrate the guest group, and how can we protect our pastor from being inundated with problems from the guest group?

Remember, the role of the host pastor is to shepherd his own flock (this is discussed in chapter 9). The role of the guest pastor is to administrate the guest church. By prior agreement between the host and guest pastors, they will discuss any problems that pop up during the week at their regular scheduled meeting. From that meeting should come the process to solve any problems that may have arisen.

7. Do we have to share everything with the guest group— including our kitchen?

No, only designated areas. Any areas that are to be used exclusively by the host church should be agreed upon in the Operations Covenant. In chapter 4, this issue is discussed in detail.

8. If we share our church with two other ethnic groups, how do we conduct our holiday services without a conflict?

After the first year, this potential problem will lessen, once it is agreed upon how each group will handle their holidays. By agreeing in advance to alternate the use of the affected buildings or rooms (sanctuary, fellowship hall, classrooms), you should be able to keep any conflict to a minimum.

9. Our guest group is very liberal, and we fear they will negatively influence our church. What can we do about it?

The proper way to handle this is, first, not to jump to conclusions. Only when there has been an incident that has affected the host church's ethical standards, should there be any action taken. If there are recurrent events where the integrity of the host church may be jeopardized, the leadership should be informed so that the pastors can devise a plan to protect the host church's value system from further erosion.

10. **How often should we conduct corporate worship that includes both the host and guest membership?**

This should be negotiated between the host and guest pastors and their leadership. Some churches may be obliged to have corporate worship with their guest groups regularly (monthly, quarterly, semiannually), while others only practice corporate worship once per year.

The Guest Church Pastor

1. **We are coming out of a home Bible study into sharing space with an established church for an indefinite period of time. Our concern is that they refuse to give us a lease. Should we be worried they will evict us?**

If your host pastor agrees to a covenant (Operations), then it can act as a lease, only without any legal entanglements. Since it is very unlikely that a fellow Christian church would resort to evicting you unless a serious problem developed, a lease is not needed; however, the covenant described in this book (chapter 8) will strengthen your mutual relationship to alleviate any fears.

2. **Since we pay rent, shouldn't we be entitled to put up a sign identifying our church?**

Most cities have ordinances regarding church signs, thereby restricting their construction and placement on church property. You cannot just put up a sign wherever you please. These restrictions may conflict with the host church. Additionally, the host pastor may consider how long your guest group plans on renting the allotted space and may reject your proposal on that basis. This subject is discussed in chapter 10.

3. What kind of access can I have to the sanctuary? And can I identify our culture there?

If the guest group does not have their own sanctuary, an agreement must be made with the host pastor to establish an alternating schedule for access. Ordinarily, permission must be granted in writing for extraordinary events (weddings, baptisms, etc.), while the weekly worship service and Bible study should be agreed upon and arranged in advance. When more than one ethnic group shares a church, the cultural banners, flags, posters, and various other forms of identification must be carefully selected and strategically placed in the sanctuary to avoid confusion and clutter. Some churches have teams that place and remove their cultural identification items before and after their worship service. This is done so that each group is clearly identified. Other churches blend all the cultural insignias to show the multiethnic nature of the church.

4. Is there adequate room to expand our ministry?

Naturally, this depends on the facility. In addition, the terms of occupation have a bearing on future expansion options. If your group intends to rent space from the host church for a short period (under two years), I believe the host church has no obligation to provide any future room for expansion. But if your agreement is long term (over two years), your covenant should include future expansion rights and options to accommodate any increase in membership.

5. What kind of arrangement with the host church should I expect when approaching the subject of renovations in our allotted space?

Usually, the host church will allow you to make changes that do not include structural modifications such as removing bearing walls or rewiring electric circuit-breaker boxes. Changes that include erecting partitions, minor plumbing and electrical work, and painting are not normally challenged by the host church.

Some host churches may agree to pay a portion of the cost to renovate, while others may not. This is a matter of negotiation and is discussed in chapter 5.

6. Our host church pastor has asked us to pay, in addition to our rent, a portion of the liability insurance policy on the building we occupy. Is that fair?

The premium to insure a church for liability and for property damage can be staggering. It should be expected by the guest church to pay their proportionate share of the premium for the space they rent. Some host churches factor the cost of their guest group's insurance into the rent, while others add it on top. This is a matter for negotiation between the host and guest pastors.

7. Our host pastor asked us to tell him the amount of our annual budget to determine the amount of our rent. Is that proper?

The purpose in asking is not to invade the privacy of the guest church but to validate before God the fair amount of rent to charge. There are various ways to calculate the amount of the rent to be charged to the guest group. Using the annual budget as a guide is just one of them. These various formulas are described in chapter 8.

8. What kind of Shared Expense Covenant would be best for our group?

This depends on several variable factors such as your annual budget, the amount of space you occupy, etc. This subject is discussed in length in chapter 8.

9. Should I be concerned that some of my members may defect and move over to the host church?

While initial curiosity may cause some of your members to visit the host church, be assured that no ethical host pastor is interested in taking sheep from your group. Leave them alone and they'll come home.

10. How can I befriend our host church pastor?

Pastors long for camaraderie with other pastors. In the secular world, friendships often originate and revolve around hobbies, sports or social activities, or mutual interests. There is nothing wrong with pastors finding similar common interests and allowing them to extend their friendship. The binding link, naturally, is their united relationship in the Lord.

The Guest Church Membership

1. Why is sharing a church better for us than renting a storefront?

There are several benefits to sharing a church over renting a store. The location of the storefront may not be conducive for a church where there are other commercial stores that could impact negatively on your ministry. Also, many visitors view a storefront ministry as temporary, and while they may visit, most look for a permanent-type ministry to get planted before they commit themselves. There is also the issue of the rent. When dealing with a commercial landlord or corporate holding firm, it is unlikely they will lower the rent to advance the kingdom of God. In a Christian church, the amount of space you will be able to rent will be much greater at a reduced rent.

2. Does the congregation really want us to share their church or is this just a dream between the pastors?

By the time your pastor has given you the go-ahead to move into the host church, the host congregation has already given its approval. It is very unlikely that the host pastor has not received approval from both his elected board or deacons and his congregation before notifying your pastor to come and share the church.

3. What right of appeal do we have regarding our concerns with the host church pastor and congregation?

The correct procedure for a member of the guest group to express his concerns would be first to inform his leadership, that is, a deacon or elder in his church. The chain of command dictates that the leadership should bring the concern all the way up to the pastor for him to settle.

4. Our congregation is mostly employed in the service sector of society and our membership income is low to moderate. What are we expected to do if the host church raises our rent or asks us to pay half of the renovations?

Both the rent and the cost of renovations are negotiated amounts that both the host and guest pastors need to agree on. In Christian ministry (as opposed to secular agreements), a great deal of latitude is granted in dealing with financial matters, thus enabling the guest group to feel comfortable in meeting their expenses.

5. Our host pastor severely restricts the kind of renovations we are allowed to perform ourselves in order to save money. Is that fair to us?

The guest group must realize that a number of factors prohibit nonprofessionals from making renovations on church buildings. Commercial insurance carriers will not provide protection if a claim results from faulty construction or wiring performed by unlicensed personnel. In addition, any major renovations on church property must be completed by licensed professionals and must conform to local code. Renovations such as laying carpet or painting do not fall into this category.

6. Some of our members have expressed concern that the host church is located in an undesirable neighborhood. Should that matter to us?

Of course it is important, but one must consider the purpose of the church, especially if it is located in a community (as opposed to an area church). This purpose is to reach the neighborhood for Christ—the very neighborhood where God has planted the church. It has been my experience that the church should be a sparkling example to the community or area by keeping up its appearance to maintain the church's testimony for Christ, regardless of the condition of the surrounding neighborhood. It may be that God is going to use the guest group to help with that commission.

7. Our group is composed of young families with many small children, while the host group has mostly middle-aged adults with grown children. Accordingly, there are few provisions (playground, nursery, etc.) to accommodate us. What can we do about this, assuming everything else is acceptable?

Similar issues are discussed in chapters 4 and 5. In short, this is a matter for negotiation between the host and guest pastors. In most cases, the renovation expenses should be shared.

8. What efforts can we take to encourage camaraderie and fellowship with the host congregation?

Apart from having periodic corporate worship services to encourage fellowship, having corporate prayer meetings and Bible studies should also be considered. Then there are social functions such as combined luncheons (or picnics on the church grounds), together with fun events such as ball games, to promote camaraderie.

9. Will the women of our congregation be able to collaborate with the women of the host congregation over special events such as holiday functions, receptions, and social affairs?

Despite the language barrier (assuming there are ethnic differences), there is no reason why both the host and guest church women should not collaborate over special events. For the most part, women play an important role in initiating conversation and arranging events that can turn into an opportunity for both host and guest groups to get to know one another better. For this reason, both the host and guest pastor should encourage and promote the women working together to coordinate special events.

10. As leaders in our guest group who influence the rank-
and-file members, what can we do to promote a feeling
of ownership in the host church?

The role of spiritual leaders is extremely important in the
church since the membership will usually follow in their
footsteps. First, the congregation needs to know that both
the host and guest pastor are on the same page. Both the
host and guest leaders should promote unity among themselves at all times; if the leadership is divided, what can we
expect of the congregations? Second, guest leaders should
set the example to their congregation by demonstrating a
kindred spirit toward the host congregation. This includes
avoiding negative conversations about the host group and
being available to help them whenever possible.

When the guest leaders treat the host church property with
respect, they promote ownership in the ministry by virtue
of the fact that they make a statement of investment. They
treat the facility as if it were their own.

Notes

Chapter 1—Why Should You Share Your Church?

1. G. W. Bromiley, "Unity," in Walter A. Elwell, *Evangelical Dictionary of Theology* (Grand Rapids: Baker, 1994), 1,127.

Chapter 2—United We Stand

1. James S. Hewett, *Illustrations Unlimited* (Wheaton: Tyndale House, 1988), 125–26.

2. J. Campbell White, "The Laymen's Missionary Movement," in *Perspectives on the World Christian Movement* (Pasadena, Calif.: William Carey Library, 1992), B-93.

3. Friedrich Hanck, "Fellowship," in *Wycliffe Bible Encyclopedia* (Oak Harbor, Wash.: Logos Bible Research, 1997), 789–809.

4. Quoted on http://www.brainyquote.com.

5. David Levy, *The Tabernacle: Shadows of the Messiah* (The Friends of Israel Gospel Ministry, 1993).

6. Ralph D. Winter, "The New Macedonia," in *Perspectives on the World Christian Movement* (Pasadena, Calif.: William Carey Library, 1992).

Chapter 5—Agreeing on Renovations

1. James D. Berkley, ed., *Leadership Handbooks of Practical Theology*, vol. 3 (Grand Rapids: Baker, 1994), 367.

2. Ibid., 368.

3. Ibid., 368.

4. Ibid., 369.

Chapter 6—Guests Are Looking for Practical Answers

1. Pastor Mike was allowed to use the auditorium, three classrooms, and two rest rooms.

2. Ministry groups in transition that rent schools while their church building is being constructed are an exception to these considerations.

3. Rick Warren, *The Purpose-Driven Church* (Grand Rapids: Zondervan, 1995), 65.

Chapter 7—Guests Are Looking for Scriptural Answers

1. Walter A. Elwell, ed., *Evangelical Dictionary of Biblical Theology* (Grand Rapids: Baker Books, 1996).
2. Ibid.
3. Ibid.
4. Ibid.
5. Ibid.
6. Millard J. Erickson, *Christian Theology* (Grand Rapids: Baker, 1992), 1,038.
7. Charles R. Swindoll, *The Tale of the Tardy Oxcart* (Nashville: Word, 1998), 599.
8. Erickson, *Christian Theology*, 1,133.

Chapter 8—Is Shaking Hands Enough?

1. From the Operations Covenant between North Pompano Baptist Church and First Brazilian Baptist Church entitled "Spatial Parameters."
2. Ralph F. Wilson, "How to Share Your Buildings without Losing Your Church," Christian Articles Archive (on-line services, October 27, 2000).
3. Stig Hanson, *The Unity of the Church in the New Testament: Colossians and Ephesians* (Lexington, Ky.: American Theological Library Association, 1963), 107–8.
4. James D. Berkley, ed., *Leadership Handbooks of Practical Theology*, vol. 3 (Grand Rapids: Baker, 1994), 370.
5. Ralph F. Wilson, adaptation from "How to Share Your Buildings without Losing Your Church," Christian Articles Archive (on-line services, October 27, 2000).
6. The Shared Expense Covenant can be a separate written document from the Operations Covenant or a codicil to it. A verbal agreement will not promote tranquility in ministry and should be avoided.
7. The rental agreement should carry a clause that allows for increases. The following is an extract from the NPBC Operations Covenant: "The leadership of NPBC and FBBC (First Brazilian Baptist Church) meet in early December of each year to discuss the amount of rent for the following year. Discussion by the NPBC church council and the leadership of FBBC will precede any rent increase. The items determining any increase in rent will be mutually agreed upon by both NPBC and FBBC."
8. Taken from the NPBC concept of Shared Expense Covenant.
9. Proportionate insurance expense determined by insurance agent according to percentage of facility occupied by guest ministry.
10. Common areas: main sanctuary, carpets, air conditioners, fellowship hall, outside courtyards, etc.
11. Guest occupied areas: the buildings or rooms used exclusively by the guest ministry. They would include areas such as their administrative office building or room, classrooms, etc.

12. Designated areas: Those areas not occupied by the guest church, but used primarily by them. They would include children's playground/equipment; shelters for their special events, etc.

13. Samuel Chadwick, *The Way to Pentecost* (Berne, Ind.: Light and Hope Publications, 1937), 29–30.

Chapter 9—Setting Boundaries to Minimize Conflicts

1. Richard R. Hammar, *Pastor, Church & Law* (Matthews, N.C.: Christian Ministry Resources, 2000), 482.

Chapter 10—Dealing with the Church Sign

1. James D. Berkley, ed., *Leadership Handbooks of Practical Theology*, vol. 3 (Grand Rapids: Baker, 1994), 384–85.

2. Ibid.

3. John Throop in Berkley, *Leadership Handbooks*, 384–85.

Chapter 11—Maintaining Your Identity as the Host Church

1. George Barna, *The Power of Vision* (Ventura, Calif.: Gospel Light, 1997), 45.

2. Extract taken from Ministry Vision for North Pompano Baptist Church.

3. Mission statement of the North Pompano Baptist Church.

4. *Nelson's Illustrated Bible Dictionary* (PC Study Bible, ver. 3, Biblesoft, Seattle, WA).

5. Rick Warren, *The Purpose-Driven Church* (Grand Rapids: Zondervan, 1998), 98.

6. This list is not exhaustive but does provide reference points for further exploration.

Chapter 12—Where Are You Going and How Do You Get There?

1. Rick Warren, *The Purpose-Driven Church* (Grand Rapids: Zondervan, 1998), 100.

Chapter 13—When to Call In a Mediator

1. Because of the nature of the rental agreement made with the former pastor, our church was fully within its rights to require that this group pay for the expenses on the building they were renting.

2. Samuel Chadwick, *The Way to Pentecost* (Berne, Ind.: Light and Hope Publications, 1937), 7.

3. Jim Cymbala, *Fresh Power* (Grand Rapids: Zondervan, 2001), 187.

4. James D. Berkley, ed., *Leadership Handbooks of Practical Theology*, vol. 3 (Grand Rapids: Baker, 1994), 197.

5. Jay E. Adams, *The Christian Counselor's Manual* (Grand Rapids: Zondervan, 1973), 52.

Chapter 14—Asking Your Guests to Leave

1. Ralph F. Wilson, "How to Share Your Buildings without Losing Your Church," Christian Articles Archive (on-line services, October 27, 2000).

2. Both Luther and Calvin agree that 2 Cor. 8:18–19 is referring to Barnabas, indicating, therefore, subsequent joint work.

Chapter 15—Sharing Your Church as a New Pastor

1. James D. Berkley, ed., *Leadership Handbooks of Practical Theology*, vol. 3 (Grand Rapids: Baker, 1994), 119.
2. Rick Warren, *The Purpose-Driven Church* (Grand Rapids: Zondervan, 1995), 96.
3. Merrill F. Unger et al., *The New Unger's Bible Dictionary* (Chicago: Moody Press, 1988).
4. James Bryant Conant quoted on http://encyclopedia.com.
5. Jay E. Adams, *The Christian Counselor's Manual* (Grand Rapids: Zondervan, 1973), 414.
6. James D. Berkley, ed., *Leadership Handbooks of Practical Theology*, vol. 3, 136.

Chapter 16—The Joy of Sharing Worship Together

1. As of this writing, September 21, 2001, the attack on the World Trade Center is only ten days old. Our nation, along with other countries, is still reeling from the disaster by desperately reaching out to one another, to console and comfort the countless hearts that have been broken by this awful outpouring of hate. It is a divine opportunity for the body of Christ to show its unity by sharing with its community of fellow human beings, its hope and faith in Christ's salvation.
2. Robert L. Saucy, *The Church in God's Program* (Chicago: Moody, 1972), 93.
3. Samuel Chadwick, *The Way to Pentecost* (Berne, Ind.: Light and Hope Publications, 1937), 11–13.
4. Jim Cymbala, *Fresh Power* (Grand Rapids: Zondervan, 2001), 45.
5. Charles Colson, *Kingdoms in Conflict* (Grand Rapids: William Morrow/Zondervan, 1987), 75.
6. Chadwick, *The Way to Pentecost*, 94.
7. Cymbala, 66.
8. The Brazilian pastor speaks relatively good English in conversation but prefers to preach in his native tongue.
9. C. S. Lewis, in Edythe Draper, *Draper's Book of Quotations for the Christian World* (Wheaton: Tyndale, 1992), entry number 11493.

Chapter 17—Making a Statement in Your Community

1. Mother Teresa quoted in *REACH*, vol. 27, no. 4 (Grand Rapids: Christian Reformed Home Missions, 2001).
2. Ralph F. Wilson, "Why Do People Attend Church?," Christian Articles Archive (on-line services, July 23, 2001).
3. Francis A. Schaeffer quoted in *REACH*, vol. 27, no. 1 (Grand Rapids: Christian Reformed Home Missions, 2001).
4. Charles Colson, *Kingdoms in Conflict* (Grand Rapids: William Morrow/Zondervan, 1987), 181.

Chapter 18—The Future Outlook of the American Church

1. George Barna, "Goals and Priorities" (Barna Research Online, Sept. 28, 2001).

2. George Barna, "Concerns, Needs, Challenges" (Barna Research Online, Sept. 28, 2001).

3. Lance R. Barker, "The Rural Church: Its Future Challenges" (www.Web-minister.com, Sept. 29, 2001).

4. George Barna, "Americans Describe Their Ideal Church" (Barna Research Online, October 1998).

5. Jim Cymbala, *Fresh Power* (Grand Rapids: Zondervan, 2001), 123.

6. Peter Wagner, "The Homogeneous Unit Principle" in James D. Berkley, ed., *Leadership Handbooks of Practical Theology*, vol. 2 (Grand Rapids: Baker, 1994), 35.

7. Charles Colson, *Kingdoms in Conflict* (Grand Rapids: Zondervan, 1987), 102.

8. Barna defines the unchurched adult (eighteen or older) as one who has not attended a Christian church service within the past six months, not including a holiday service (such as Easter or Christmas) or a special event at a church (such as a wedding or funeral). "Unchurched People" (Barna Research Online, Sept. 28, 2001).

9. Ibid.

10. George Barna quoted in *REACH*, vol. 27, no. 5 (Grand Rapids: Christian Reformed Home Missions, Sept. 2001).

Dr. Curtin, originally from Long Island, New York, relocated to South Florida in 1987 to direct a large Christian ministry with its focus on Jewish evangelism. Within three years he resumed his ministerial studies, earning a B.S. and M.A. in Biblical Studies from Trinity Evangelical Divinity School in Deerfield, Illinois. From there he went on to earn a Doctor of Ministry degree in Christian Counseling from the South Florida Bible College and Theological Seminary in Deerfield Beach, Florida, where he presided as Academic Dean and professor of Biblical Studies. Dr. Curtin is also an adjunct professor for Trinity College in Miami in addition to teaching for the Moody Bible Institute External Studies program. He and his helpmate of thirty-seven years, Kathy, presently share the ministry of serving the Lord in the pastorate. They have three married children and five grandchildren.

His first book, *The False Hope,* a work of prophetic fiction, was published by Briarwood and is in its second year of publication. His second book of prophetic fiction, *Ancient Lights,* dramatizes the modern discovery of the ancient biblical priestly device, the Urim and Thummim, and its role in the emergence of the Antichrist. This book will soon be published by Destiny Image Publishers.

His pastoral counseling experience led him to write in a different genre, Christian counseling. *Hope for the Hurting Heart* is designed to aid the family of God in times of need. He is presently seeking publication for this completed labor of love as well.

This book, *Sharing Your Church Building,* is a work of the author's passion for the pastorate and his love for shepherding people. God has asked him to lead three culturally divergent ministries under one banner in the Christian church, and his experiences should prove to be a valuable tool in the hands of the body of Christ.